Acceptance, Understanding, and the Moral Imperative of Promoting Social Justice Education in the Schoolhouse

Nicholas D. Young

Elizabeth Jean

Teresa A. Citro

Series in Education

VERNON PRESS

Copyright © 2019 Vernon Press, an imprint of Vernon Art and Science Inc, on behalf of the author.

All rights reserved. No part of this publication may be reproduced, stored in a retrieval system, or transmitted in any form or by any means, electronic, mechanical, photocopying, recording, or otherwise, without the prior permission of Vernon Art and Science Inc.

www.vernonpress.com

In the Americas:
Vernon Press
1000 N West Street,
Suite 1200, Wilmington,
Delaware 19801
United States

In the rest of the world:
Vernon Press
C/Sancti Espiritu 17,
Malaga, 29006
Spain

Series in Education

Library of Congress Control Number: 2019933347

ISBN: 978-1-62273-730-7

Also available:
Hardback: 978-1-62273-623-2
E-book: 978-1-62273-644-7

Product and company names mentioned in this work are the trademarks of their respective owners. While every care has been taken in preparing this work, neither the authors nor Vernon Art and Science Inc. may be held responsible for any loss or damage caused or alleged to be caused directly or indirectly by the information contained in it.

Every effort has been made to trace all copyright holders, but if any have been inadvertently overlooked the publisher will be pleased to include any necessary credits in any subsequent reprint or edition.

Cover design by Vernon Press using elements designed by Freepik.

Table of Contents

Acknowledgement   v

Preface   vii

Chapter One
**Social Justice as a Teaching Construct:
Fundamentals Under Review**   1
  Nicholas D. Young, *American International College*
  Jennifer Innocenti, *American International College*
  Elizabeth Jean, *Endicott College*

Chapter Two
**Home-School Partnerships: Connecting
with Families through a Social Justice Lens**   11
  Elizabeth Jean, *Endicott College*
  Nicholas D. Young, *American International College*

Chapter Three
**School Law and Policy:
Promoting and Protecting Diverse Students**   23
  Jennifer A. Smolinski, *American International College*

Chapter Four
**Gender and Sexual Orientation:
Understanding the Differences Among Students**   37
  Elizabeth Jean, *Endicott College*
  Doris L. Buckley, *Northern Essex Community College*

Chapter Five
**Reaching and Teaching Adoptees in the Classroom:
Making All Feel Welcome**   49
  Karen Russo, *St. Joseph's College, New York*

Chapter Six
**Racial, Ethnic, and Linguistic Diversity:
Meeting Students Where They Are** 61
   Charles B. Hutchison,
   The University of North Carolina at Charlotte
   Jonimay Morgan,
   The University of North Carolina at Charlotte
   Michelle Pass,
   The University of North Carolina at Charlotte

Chapter Seven
**Advancing the Social Standing of Students from
Educationally At-Risk Populations: Students Who
Learn, Look, Speak, Behave, or Believe Differently** 75
   Ellen L. Duchaine, *Texas State University*

Chapter Eight
**Understanding and Addressing Bias in
Classroom Assessment: Promoting Fairness
Through Equitable Grading Practices** 93
   Nicholas D. Young, *American International College*
   Dianne M. Young, *University of Massachusetts*

Chapter Nine
**Teaching to the Common Core State Standards
While Emphasizing Social Justice:
Classroom Strategies and Practices That Work** 105
   Kristi L. Santi, *University of Houston*
   Jacqueline Hawkins, *University of Houston*
   Sara J. Jones, *University of Houston*

Chapter Ten
**College Preparation and Professional Development:
What Every Preservice and Veteran Teacher Should
Know About Social Justice Education** 119
   Nicholas D. Young, *American International College*
   Jennifer Innocenti, *American International College*

List of Acronyms 131

About the Primary Authors 133

Acknowledgement

It is a pleasure to use this opportunity to thank Sue Clark for her tremendous contributions to this book as our chief editor. She has unmatched wordsmithing skills and a pleasant demeanor that make her a wonderful colleague on all of our projects. May our readers know that she is the "talent behind the curtain"; and she knows that we are grateful for all she does to make our words shine.

Preface

Acceptance, Understanding, and the Moral Imperative of Promoting Social Justice Education in the Schoolhouse examines the critical issues associated with the topic of social justice in preschool through grade 12 (P-12) education. This book is most appropriate for preservice and veteran teachers, school and educational psychologists, related special education service professionals, educational administrators, guidance counselors, graduate education professors, policy-makers, parents and student leaders who wish to gain a better understanding of how social justice can and should become a valuable part of the educational landscape.

Understanding the challenges related to educational inequity requires a comprehensive and systematic re-examination of educational reform; more specifically, this book defines social justice education, offers different perspectives from major thought leaders, and examines the challenges faced by different populations when it comes to receiving equal opportunity and treatment. Emphasis will be placed on programs, approaches, and strategies to increasingly teach tolerance, respect, and understanding within and between these groups and members of the majority culture. The focus, then, will be educational practices designed to prepare students from diverse backgrounds to be active, contributing, and fully participatory members of our contemporary society.

Our motivation for writing this book arose due to...

- Our concern that due to race, ethnicity, gender, socioeconomic status, and so many other indicators, all students in America are not given the same opportunities in school;
- Our belief that helping educators understand and implement social justice in the classroom will increase the equity between students;
- Our awareness that equity in the classroom is the first step to more positive social and academic outcomes throughout a school career;
- Our knowledge that students are our greatest hope for the future and providing them with equitable opportunities in

school will lead them towards a more productive and fulfilling life;
- Our sense that the world is ready for change and that social justice offers educators a platform from which to teach all students using a reflective and collaborative format.

The authors have had many occupations throughout their lives including parenting, teaching in the P-12 classroom, leadership roles in both P-12 and postsecondary, and teaching at the college and graduate levels for a combined total of over seventy-five years. This has led to many opportunities to engage with others and collaborate on best practices for all students, which have given way to many conversations about equity and social justice. The authors are proud to support the next generation of educators and students in teaching fairly and helping students become the best versions of themselves.

Social justice education in the classroom has the ability to develop students to become more thoughtful and understanding of diverse people, personalities, abilities, and struggles. Teachers are poised to be the beacon that lights the way for all students through classroom strategies and action-oriented approaches that produce positivity, collaboration, and opportunity. The chapters in this book reflect an understanding of the fundamentals of social justice as well as federal law. The many faces of students who are best served by a social justice curriculum are considered as well as how the curriculum dovetails with the Common Core State Standards and how a fair assessment process is important to student success and confidence. In a world that is complex and fraught with ambiguity and insecurity, social justice education can assist the educator, parent, professor, and student in a new relationship with the world where equity in education and opportunity in life are the norm, not just a concept.

Chapter One

Social Justice as a Teaching Construct: Fundamentals Under Review

Nicholas D. Young, *American International College*

Jennifer Innocenti, *American International College*

Elizabeth Jean, *Endicott College*

The term social justice has been tossed around in education and used in mission statements, goals, job announcements, education reform proposals, curricula, and visions; however, there is a lack of understanding and a limited collective definition of social justice due to its overuse (Hytten & Bettez, 2011). In fact, it is probably easier to agree on defining and identifying social injustices (Chung & Bemak, 2012). Social injustice is the unfair treatment or inequities that have developed due to 'isms' such as racism, sexism, religion, ableism, as well as socioeconomic status, sexual orientation, and social issues that include the individual, family, local, national and global communities (Chung & Bemak, 2012). 'Isms' are defined by Merriam-Webster (2018) as "an oppressive and especially discriminatory attitude or belief [or] prejudice or discrimination on the basis of a (specified) attribute" (n.p.). Social justice, therefore, refers to fairness and equity for all people at all times (Chung & Bemak, 2012; Hytten & Bettez, 2011; Mthethwa-Sommers, 2014).

Background of Social Justice Theory

Social justice theory is derived from and rooted in the theory of social transmission theory, which states that educators must imitate and maintain the current "socio-economic and political structure [or status quo of the] dominant group's desired cultural traditions, beliefs, and values from one generation to the next" (Mthethwa-Sommers, 2014, p. 7). Social transmission theory can be broken down into functionalism and structural functionalism yet, they are largely the same. For the purposes of this discussion, they are one and the same with a focus on education.

Structural functionalism postulates that its purpose is to maintain homeostasis, and functionalism is much the same. The combined belief is that educational institutions/schools should maintain and imitate the dominant group's status quo, which is accomplished using a three-pronged approach in which the first objective is to "teach values that abet uncritical patriotism, encourage un-scrutinized acceptance of laws and rules, and instill obedience of all authority figures and power representatives" (Mthethwa-Sommers, 2014, p. 8). This ensures that there is a minimal risk posed by those that simply comply and conform to the expectations of authority figures. The second objective is to "facilitate assimilation of students into a single national culture or the dominant culture" (Mthethwa-Sommers, 2014, p. 8). Functionalists believe that schools should essentially make clones, meaning that when a person has graduated from the school system, they should possess values and beliefs that mirror the single national culture.

The third objective is to identify the students' academic ability and categorize the students based on their academic ability. Once academic ability is identified, teachers are encouraged to steer students in the direction that represents the greatest potential. A high achieving student, for example, should be steered to more leadership occupations, while a mediocre or low achieving student should be steered towards occupations that are menial; thus, allowing an equal proportion of job placement and encouraging a status quo (Mthethwa-Sommers, 2014).

Social Justice Theory and Contradiction

Chinn (2014) argued that social justice education theory serves two contradictory purposes; one is to sustain culture, while the other is to challenge and change culture. It is both a process and a goal for the school and social justice theory; therefore, it is a means to sustain existing culture, while also embracing a move towards democracy that encourages the acceptance of the ideological, cultural, religious, and social diversity (Bassey, 2016). The goal of social justice education theory can be summed up as the equal participation of all groups in society, meeting the needs of all students by providing equal distribution of resources, and facilitating a physically and psychologically safe and secure environment for all students (Mthethwa-Sommers, 2014).

The term social justice theory is a continuum as much as an umbrella; thus, it continuously adapts as more theories (i.e., critical theory, critical race theory, critical theory classrooms, multicultural education theory, postmodern theory, post-structural theory, feminist, and lessons for teacher education) are developed (Mthethwa-Sommers, 2014). Each theory begins with its own perception and definition and develops objectives and goals that may pose as a contradiction to social justice education theory; yet, a driving pledge of all social justice education theories is the demand that institutions are to unveil and transform oppressive policies and practices (Hytten & Bettez, 2011; Mthethwa-Sommers, 2014).

The Perspective of Social Justice-Oriented Educators

Social justice-oriented educators consider the values and politics that influence institutions, while further considering equitable ways to organize the school and teach in a socially just manner (Hytten, 2015). These educators tackle tough questions by acknowledging current common-sense practices as well as identifying inequalities such as race, class, gender, and language, among others. Social justice-oriented advocates note that there may be unequal social relations and inequalities on both an individual and systemic level; however, educators attempt to utilize their position by imagining and understanding what it would be like to face inequalities and how to better serve fairness and equity through resolutions (Hytten, 2015). This aspect may be difficult for dominant group educators despite attempting to remain unbiased in the classroom.

Promoters of social justice believe in a broad social purpose that prepares students to use knowledge and analytical skills to identify different and more effective ways that schools and social institutions can treat people in a more humane and fair manner (Hytten, 2015). Advocates work towards a more ingrained view of social justice education that includes praising diversity, ensuring that all students feel valued, critiquing information, and distributing resources fairly and equally (Hytten, 2015). For this vision to be achieved, social justice education must be supported by equity, activism, and social literacy. Equity is defined as students having fair access to educational experiences that are both challenging and enriching. Activism incorporates democratic citizenship from students to change the future of education. It is important to note that social justice education "does not inherently involve teaching information in one-sided ways, indoctrinating students into specific worldviews or ignoring the importance of skill development" (Hytten, 2015, p. 3). Social literacy includes nourishing connections and relationships, challenging oppression, and acting with courage (Hytten, 2015).

Social justice-oriented educators need to be activists who foster the values, visions, and beliefs that help students develop habits critical for democratic citizenship such as critical thinking, compassion, responsibility, open-mindedness, care, and respect (Hytten, 2015). Hytten (2015) noted that teaching social justice in the classroom can be both a fine line and a grey area, as the educator must leave all personal and political agendas out of the classroom and be the model for students. Educators must do more than simply read from the text; rather, it is vital that personal anecdotes are used to make the material relatable for the students. Chinn (2014) argued that many students read the text and can follow or even regurgitate the text, but often students do not seem to question what is in print. Teachers also influence how a student receives the information, which may be dependent on the style of delivery, the student's learning style, a disability or an academic struggle (Bassey, 2016). When a teacher reflects on what is missing in a text, often it is a missing social element. When encouraging students to think about missing social factors, they may be able to verbally recognize the errors, but struggle to put the ideas on paper (Chinn, 2014). Teachers foster how students should think about learning, how they develop opinions or beliefs, respond to others, and see their place in the world (Hytten, 2015). As a proponent of social justice, teachers can ensure that classroom advocacy includes valuing and respecting all students; therefore, eliminating the possibility that a student may feel alienated, oppressed, silenced, or otherwise harmed.

Along with instilling democratic citizenship, social justice teachers must remain neutral, while 'ethically' uphold their vision and stance of a good education (Hytten, 2015). Social justice-oriented educators must encourage students to "develop democratic habits, alleviate suffering, cultivate critical consciousness, sustain diversity, and create more humane social relationships" (Hytten, 2015, p. 1). Remaining as neutral as possible eliminates personal practices, ethics, and virtues that may taint the social justice platform; although all teachers are partisan in one way or another and have their own bias (Gunzenhauser, 2015; Hytten, 2015). Objectivity, worldviews, and viewpoints are passed on through teaching as texts, activities, assignments, lessons, and grades as well as the trust, rapport, and relationships that are built are decisions and expectations that come from the educator, much of which is based on opinion (Hytten, 2014).

The National Education Association (2018) code of ethics that indicates the expected commitments to be made to students. Teachers are encouraged to promote democratic values and citizenship, encourage independent thinking, consider multiple perspectives, and keep students safe. On the other hand, educators should not distort any viewpoints deliberately nor should they embarrass or disparage students intentionally (The National Education Association, 2018). It is the educators' duty to protect a students' rights and federal protections as well as to keep confidential, student information (The National Education Association, 2018).

While maintaining a neutral viewpoint in the classroom as a social justice educator, it is important to develop and sustain ongoing ethical relationships by reflecting on a personal philosophy of education. Teachers must think ahead to their desired outcome and reflect on the means, methods, and ways in which they can create a safe and secure learning environment based on the principles of social justice (Hytten, 2015).

Pedagogy: Social Justice Teaching

According to Dover (2009), there are six principles of social justice education that positively impact students' behavioral, motivational, attitudinal, and academic outcomes to include

(1) *Assume all students are participants in knowledge construction, have high expectations for students and themselves, and foster learning communities;*
(2) *Acknowledge, value, and build upon students' existing knowledge, interest, cultural and linguistic resources;*
(3) *Teach specific academic skills and bridge gaps in students' learning;*
(4) *Work in reciprocal partnership with students' families and communities;*
(5) *Critique and employ multiple forms of assessment; and*
(6) *Explicitly teach about activism, power, and inequality in schools and society* (p. 510).

Social justice education theory assumes that teachers must possess high expectations not only for their students but for themselves while promoting academic achievement and skills and fostering a safe and secure learning environment (Dover, 2009; National Association of School Psychologists. (2013).

Minority students, or those of color, may struggle with their social identity as well as perceived negativity from not meeting the teacher's expectations; however, when the teacher has high expectations for all students equally, students were found to excel in academic ventures (Dover, 2009). Taking it a step further, when teachers felt responsible for student learning, they were more likely to promote more equitable and effective learning environments (Dover, 2009). Democratic citizenship, therefore, is a product of a safe and secure learning environment that fosters social and academic cooperation along with self-confidence, motivation, a sense of belonging, and engagement (OECD, 2018; National Association of School Psychologists, 2013).

Social justice-oriented teachers must also engage families to help foster curriculum that is culturally responsive - especially for English as a Second Language students (Dover, 2009). Students whose families participated and engaged in the classroom were reported to have improved grade point averages, were able to meet the academic achievement standards, improved literacy development, set educational goals, and were more likely to graduate college (Grant & Ray, 2016). Families of diverse cultures who were active in the school and classroom were able to share about their personal rituals, beliefs, and customs; thus, the teacher understood more, and the teacher-family-student relationship was improved (Dover, 2009; Epstein & Sanders, 2019).

Social justice-oriented teachers who create a culturally responsive environment in the classroom are able to build on the educational foundation and interests of the students and connect learning to the students' life outside of school (Bassey, 2016; Jean & Rotas, 2019). Research has found that maintaining a culturally responsive and sociocultural-centered teaching style has positively impacted student participation, achievement, self-esteem, connectedness (sense of belonging), motivation, social identity, and reduced stereotypical attitudes of minority students (Dover, 2009; Hytten, 2015). Using culturally responsive materials in the classroom, student learning opportunities have increased as they connect new information to existing knowledge.

Culturally sensitive teaching has been found to have a significant impact on minority students, while teachers who resist culturally sensitive teaching limit the positive experiences and knowledge of students (Dover, 2009). Teachers who resist teaching using social justice principles might cause some students to refuse to engage with others who are viewed as "different" as well as promote microaggression and violence against minority students (Gunzenhauser, 2015). A quasi-experimental study conducted by Hughes and colleagues (2004) found that culturally sensitive/responsive teaching had positive effects on student outcomes, both individually and as a group. Students in this study were more on-task, had better attitudes about school, spent more time on both teacher- and student-led instructional activities, engaged in more learning opportunities; and were given higher quality instructions (Hughes et al., 2004).

Hytten (2015) argued that teachers who pushed for social justice-oriented curriculum helped students by learning to think critically, engaged students in considering diverse perspectives, were able to value students' linguistic and cultural resources and were able to get the students more involved in the community. Teachers and communities that engaged in social justice outside of the classroom encouraged students by listening to them, held them to higher expectations, provided more options, and cared more about their success (Hytten, 2015). These behaviors are influenced by the ethics and moral characteristics of the teacher-student relationship. Hawkins (2015) argued that teaching practices are intrinsically entwined with any issues that relate to what is considered good, virtuous, right, and caring in a teacher's actions, personhood, and relationships with others.

Educators who believe in social justice-oriented teaching argue that the central purpose of schooling is to create the habits necessary to make true democracy a reality, meaning that they strive to empower students to understand the world around them (Hawkins, 2015). Students learn to identify problems and their root causes, cultivate imagination, and collaborate with others in transforming societies so that all people can live fulfilling lives (Hytten, 2015). A teacher must cultivate mutual respect among students by modeling respectful responses to opinions that may differ from others (Gunzenhauser, 2015). This may provide a moment of understanding in what could otherwise be a contentious misunderstanding between two students.

Personal Reflection

One of the best methods to address biases, ethics, and morals is through personal reflection (Hytten, 2015). Teachers need to uphold virtues such as honesty, dedication, fairness, compassion, care, constancy, practical wisdom, diligence, personal responsibility, patience, respect, integrity, courage, trustworthiness, empathy, civility, kindness, beneficence, and conscientiousness in the classroom. These can be separated into three areas of character, intellect, and care. Character includes reflective humility, intellect represents open-mindedness, and sympathetic attentiveness is a form of caring (Hytten, 2015).

Hytten (2015) notes that self-reflection leads to good character traits such as sincerity, self-knowledge, trustworthiness, persistence, courage, and perseverance. When individuals are self-reflective with a critical eye, they are able to explore personal choices and beliefs from different viewpoints and will be open to engage in sensitive dialogue. During critical self-reflection, the individual is able to identify feelings and moments when they become defensive or frustrated and can honestly challenge current beliefs. Reflective humility, therefore, requires an open heart, open mind, and vulnerability while listening to others (Hytten, 2015).

According to Hytten (2015), scholars believe open-mindedness is an intellectual attitude that is an art because it requires the person to listen to multiple perspectives, taking ample time to consider alternative explanations and facts, and being able to recognize the possibility of error in our own way of thinking. As teachers gain knowledge about social justice and cultural sensitivity, it challenges all previous experiences and beliefs. It is easy to find scholars who share similar viewpoints and beliefs, thus never challenging oneself. Scholars have identified several questions that they can ask themselves to make a determination about really being open-minded: Do I remind students not to take my word as gospel but to consult other sources of information?; Do I identify moments where I am uncertain about ideas or call attention to the controversial nature of some positions?; Am I transparent about the ways I have shaped the curriculum as well as accept feedback?; Do I read other diverse perspectives that do not share my original beliefs?; Do I pose genuine questions or simply ask questions to elicit a desired response, and do I listen respectfully to student questions or do I prefer ready-made student responses from questionnaires?

Lastly, sympathetically attentive is when a teacher tries to understand others' experiences and see things from their point of view despite finding their beliefs problematic. Sympathetic attentiveness is a form of caring because it is putting an emphasis on caring for someone else and truly wanting to help them and make a difference. Caring is more than holding good intentions, being kind and supportive; rather it is about being in the moment with another person and listening to his or her story, to include needs, culture, and context.

Final Thoughts

Social justice-oriented educators bring up areas that call for change, making it a somewhat uncomfortable topic at times (Gunzenhauser, 2015). Dialogue needs to be open, authentic, educational, and informative to challenge oppression, social, political, and economic structure, and stereotypes (Gunzenhauser, 2015). Social justice-oriented teachers should ensure the family is included whenever possible, as this promotes academic achievement as well as a deeper firsthand knowledge about the students, their beliefs, and culture (Dover, 2009). It is vital that the educator has students participate in the study of all cultures (Kumagai & Lypson, 2009). A P-12 curriculum with a focus on social justice is often a good place to begin; however, there are specific principles that will positively impact students' behavioral, motivational, attitudinal, and academic outcomes (Dover, 2009). Educators who use a reflective practice will find the most benefit in social justice education.

Points to Remember

- *The goal of social justice theory is to promote equal participation of all groups in society, meet the needs of all students by providing equal distribution of resources, and facilitate a physically and psychologically safe and secure environment for all students and promotes democratic citizenship such as critical thinking, compassion, responsibility, open-mindedness, care, and respect.*
- *Teachers are encouraged to remain neutral in their teaching methods by being aware of their biases, ethics, and morals. Educators must use a self-reflective practice in order to best help students.*
- *Teachers should have high expectations for their students as well as for themselves and model appropriate behavior and responses that encourage cultural sensitivity and reduce microaggression and violence.*
- *Educators should feel a responsibility for student learning to include an effective and equitable environment and family involvement.*

References

Bassey, M.O. (2016). *Culturally responsive teaching: Implications for educational justice.* DOI: 10.3390/educsi6040035

Chinn, P.L. (2014). Educating for social justice. *Journal of Nursing Education, 53*(9), 487. DOI: 10.3928/01484834-20140821-10

Chung, R.C.Y., Bemak, F.P. (2012). *Social justice counseling: the next steps beyond multiculturalism.* Thousand Oaks, CA: Sage.

Dover, A.G. (2009). Teaching for social justice and K-12 student outcomes: a conceptual framework and research review. *Equity & Excellence in Education, 42*(4), 507-525. DOI: 10.1080/10665680903196339

Epstein, J.L. & Sanders, M.G. (2019). *School, family, and community partnerships: Your handbook for action* (4th ed.). Thousand Oaks, CA: Corwin

Grant, K.B. & Ray, J.A. (2016). *Home, school, and community collaboration: Culturally responsive family engagement* (3rd ed.). Thousand Oaks, CA: SAGE

Gunzenhauser, M.G. (2015). Enacting social justice ethically: individual and communal habits. *Democracy & Education, 23*(2), 1-6. Retrieved from https://democracyeducationjournal.org/cgi/viewcontent.cgi?article=1238&context=home

Hawkins, B.D. (2015). The 'moral value' of teaching: the missing link in teacher preparation? *NEA Today.* Retrieved from: http://neatoday.org/2015/03/17/moral-value-teaching-missing-link-teacher-preparation/

Hughes, G. K., Cowley, K. S., Copley, L. D., Finch, N. L., Meehan, M. L., Burns, R. C., ... & Holdzkom, D. (2004). Effects of a culturally responsive teaching project on teachers and students in selected Kanawha County, WV, Schools. Retrieved from https://files.eric.ed.gov/fulltext/ED484925.pdf

Hytten, K. (2015). Ethics in teaching for democracy and social justice. *Democracy & Education, 23*(2), 1-10. Retrieved from https://democracyeducationjournal.org/home/vol23/iss2/1/

Hytten, K. & Bettez, S.C. (2011). Understanding education for social justice. *Educational Foundations, 25*(1), 7-24. Retrieved from https://files.eric.ed.gov/fulltext/EJ925898.pdf

Jean, E. & Rotas, G. (2019). Fostering growth in the classroom: Climate, culture and supports that make a difference. In N.D. Young, E. Jean, & T.A. Citro, *The Empathic Teacher:*

Learning and Applying the Principles of Social Justice Education to the Classroom, pp. 18-40. Wilmington, DE: Vernon Press.

Kumagai, A.K., & Lypson, M.L. (2009). Beyond culture competence: critical consciousness, social justice, and multicultural education. *Academic Medicine, 84*(6), 782-787. DOI: 10.1097/ACM.0b013e3181a42398

Merriam-Webster. (2018). *Isms*. Retrieved from https://www.merriam-webster.com/dictionary/ism

Mthethwa-Sommers, S. (2014). *Narratives of social justice educators: Standing firm.* New York, NY: Springer

National Association of School Psychologists. (2013). *A framework for safe and successful schools.* Retrieved from www.nasponline.org/schoolsafetyframework

National Educators' Association. (2018). *NEA 2018 handbook: Code of ethics.* Retrieved from http://www.nea.org/home/19322.htm

OECD. (2018). *Preparing our youth for an inclusive and sustainable world: The OECD PISA global competence framework.* Retrieved from https://www.oecd.org/education/Global-competency-for-an-inclusive-world.pdf

Chapter Two

Home-School Partnerships: Connecting with Families through a Social Justice Lens

Elizabeth Jean, *Endicott College*

Nicholas D. Young, *American International College*

Home-school partnerships, also called family-school partnerships, are the backbone of a student's successful educational career. Supportive and involved families are more likely to raise students who are more academically independent, attend school more regularly, and have higher graduation rates. (O'Donnell & Kirker, 2014). In addition to academics, "higher levels of family involvement participation significantly and positively predicted better student social skills and work habits" (O'Donnell & Kirker, 2014, p. 222). Equally as important, collaborative family-school relationships improve teacher effectiveness and student achievement (Castro, Exposito-Casas, Lopez-Martin, Lizasoain, Navarro-Asencio, & Gaviria, 2015; Flamboyan Foundation, 2011) There is no doubt, therefore, that students whose families are active participants in the learning process are more successful than when the family is not part of the equation.

The history of family engagement began in earnest when Lyndon B. Johnson declared a "war on poverty" in 1965 and signed the Elementary and Secondary Education Act (ESEA) into law (Paul, 2016). The ESEA sought to eliminate the gaps in poverty and education that had become a part of the American landscape. Every five years since its creation, the ESEA has been reauthorized with a variety of changes and nuances that represent the needs and wants of the government and people at that time; however, family engagement has been included in each authorization (Paul, 2016). Most recently, the Every Student Succeeds Act (ESSA) specified that schools must work to build better communication and partnerships with immediate and extended families as well as community members (Grant & Ray, 2016; Klein, 2016).

Perhaps the most important aspect of the latest reauthorization includes a caveat in which schools that receive public funding must make considerable efforts to reach families, "implement programs and provide activities that directly involve families" (Young & Jean, 2018, p. 109).

The Centers for Disease Control and Prevention (2018) define family engagement as "parents and school staff working together to support and improve the learning, development, and the health of children and adolescents" (n.p.). This shared responsibility between home and school actively supports students both in and out of school and encourages best behaviors with a focus on academic success. Teaching Tolerance (2016) reminds educators that communication that is "handled with respect and cultural sensitivity [will provide] an opportunity to live out the values of inclusiveness and equity" (p. 14). It is, therefore, essential that educators understand how to include families as they move to include social justice practices in their communication toolbox.

The Importance of Home-School Partnerships

Partnering with families is the most important collaborative experience an educator can engage in and increases the positive school experiences of both the student and the family. A strong collaborative experience between educator/school and family/student requires a positive outlook, a willingness to be open-minded, group decision making, and working together (Epstein & Sanders, 2019, Grant & Ray, 2016; Young, Jean, & Mead, 2019). This does not happen overnight; rather, the educator must take the first step in making families feel welcome in the classroom and if not, making an effort to visit the home to better understand the family (Hutchins, Greenfield, Epstein, Sanders, & Galindo, 2012; Parent Teacher Home Visit, 2016).

Families may not be familiar with such collaborations, and this makes it especially important to help them understand the dynamics of a school (McQuiggan & Megra, 2017). Many classrooms today have myriad factors that families can find either inclusive or off-putting such as technology, social-emotional dynamics, the classroom environment, and a diverse population; thus, educators must spend time creating opportunities for families to experience these things in positive ways (McQuiggan & Megra, 2017). By providing families with the information they need to understand the school and classroom, educators instantly create points of entry for families to engage. Leveraging this "family voice" (Young & Jean, 2018, p.

108) benefits the student and engages all stakeholders in valuable conversations and actions.

Understanding Family-School Partnership Frameworks

The importance of this partnership is undeniable as evidenced by a multitude of studies (Epstein & Sanders, 2018; Grant & Ray, 2016; Hutchins et al., 2012). Much of the initial work was completed by Epstein (1987) in the 1990s and early 2000 where she labeled six specific levers that create interactions and partnerships that improve relations and student outcomes. The connection levers have specific tasks associated with each one and include (1) collaborating with the community, (2) communicating, (3) decision-making, (4) volunteering, (5) learning at home, and (6) parenting (Epstein & Sanders, 2019). When these levers are put into place and used collaboratively between families and educators, students benefit with academic and behavioral growth, better attendance, and higher graduation rates (Epstein, 1987; Epstein & Sanders, 2019). Perhaps most of all, students better understand that both family and teacher are on their side and want them to succeed.

Epstein's work was updated by the Harvard Family Research Project in 2014, which Epstein oversaw (Harvard Research Project, 2014; Mapp & Kuttner, 2013). With the help of the Harvard researchers, the collaborative tools became a learning approach that included community and school resources that supported the development and learning of all students (Harvard Research Project, 2014). In addition to Epstein's model, Mapp and Kuttner (2013) created the Dual-Capacity Framework for Family-School Partnerships. Using Epstein's initial findings and levers, Mapp & Kuttner (2013) suggested that the dual-capacity framework was a "compass...to chart a path toward effective family engagement efforts that are linked to student achievement and school improvement [as opposed to Epstein's model that was a] blueprint for engagement initiatives" (p. 6).

The Dual-Capacity Framework is broken down into four essential elements to include the challenge, the opportunity conditions, policy and program goals, as well as family and staff capacity outcomes (Mapp & Kuttner, 2013).

- Challenge refers to a perceived or real lack of opportunity for partner-building activities; thus, the first step is to reimagine what types of opportunities can be created to bring families and educators together (Mapp & Kuttner, 2013; Young et al., 2019).

- Opportunity conditions refers to a list of items that are process and organizational in nature and encompass how the interactions are linked to learning or relationship building, are collaborative and interactive, are systemic across the school, integrated into all programming within the school, and sustainable with infrastructure support and resources (Mapp & Kuttner, 2013).
- Policy and program goals "build and enhance the capacity of families and staff" (U.S. Department of Education, n.d., n.p.).

Overcoming Barriers to Family-School Engagement

Barriers to engagement exist even in well-planned partnerships. On the part of the educator, some feel uninspired and that it is unnecessary to make connections, while others may have had previous negative experiences or biases that prevent them from being able to see the positives in new relationships (Grant & Ray, 2016). This same fear may belong to families who have had poor relationships with schools and teachers or who have innate biases due to past experiences. Another common barrier in this day and age is language. As more families move into the United States, this may be seen as a problem; yet, this can also be a benefit – it all depends on the perspective of those involved (Young & Jean, 2018).

It is important for both educators and families, therefore, to examine core beliefs and personal experiences and decide how to proceed. Core beliefs include an understanding that families want what is best for the student – they have a dream that includes academic success. Every family can support learning – they might just need some guidance; a partnership is equal parts educator and family, and educators and school leaders must cultivate and sustain these partnerships (Mapp, Carver, & Lander, 2017). Once these core beliefs are accepted by both sides, families and schools can work in a collaborative partnership to increase student success.

Increasing Family-School Partnerships

Armed with a basic understanding of the history and importance of family-school partnerships, school staff can bolster their ability to communicate, collaborate, and incorporate strategies and tools that will increase the connections with families and students. Considering these through a social justice lens adds another important dimension to the relationship.

Culturally Sensitive Communication

The first step in a positive family-school connection is to ensure that the teacher has given thought to the type of terminology and materials to be used (Teaching Tolerance, 2016). One way to communicate inclusiveness is to use terms such as "Dear Families" when writing home. An educator should never assume that each household contains a mother and a father as many families today are much more diverse than that and often include a grandparent, aunt, uncle, or another significant adult whose role it is to support the student (Dunifon, 2018; The Annie E. Casey Foundation, 2012). Many of these families fall under the category of kinship care, which is defined as a child who lives with an adult, blood relative or not, full-time in a "family-like relationship" (The Annie E. Casey Foundation, 2012, p. 2). Kinship care currently affects more than 2.7 million children in the United States (The Annie E. Casey Foundation, 2012).

Due to the uncertainty of family relationships, it is important for educators to understand the family dynamics and recognize the key relationships of each of their students (Teaching Tolerance, 2016). It is important to address them correctly and welcome them into the classroom and into conversations about the student. This brings into play the home language of the family and ensuring that, whenever possible, letters and information have been translated and that interpreters are available for meetings (Young, Jean & Mead, 2019). Families who see this level of commitment from teachers are bound to feel accepted and respected and show that as appreciation to the teacher.

Educators should consider the following in order to support a positive and respectful home-school relationship (1) assume that all families are partners and act with good intentions; (2) invite members to share important and interesting facts about the student, as well as hopes and dreams for the student; and (3) respect differences in family structures, cultures, and languages will exist, and view them as strengths (Teaching Tolerance, 2016). On a more personal level, teachers are encouraged to "bring a sense of self-reflectiveness and cultural humility to all conversations and interactions" (Teaching Tolerance, 2016, p. 14).

First Steps

At the beginning of the school year, there are several strategies that can help families feel more at home and wanted by the educator and the school. Visiting the home or making a positive call home are necessary first steps and may require a translator so that communication is clear. Both the call and the visit must be non-judgmental, it must be a time for both the family and the educator to share a bit about themselves and get to know one another so that a partnership can begin (Mapp et al., 2017; Parent Teacher Home Visits, 2016).

An additional event that usually takes place early during the school year is the traditional open house or back to school night. This annual event has traditionally meant that the parent sits and listens to the teacher who talks about the rules and expectations. In a positive twist, this event should instead provide an interactive component that allows the family unit to participate in an activity and should include an exit ticket with questions such as "What did you learn tonight that will help your student?", "What activities or events would be most helpful?", "What do you look forward to this year?" (Grant & Ray, 2016).

Conferences and Meetings

Having a conference or attending a meeting can cause a great deal of angst for both the educator and the family. Educators must listen carefully to what the family is saying and rephrase it to ensure they understand. Families have insights as to why the student might be struggling or having issues. In some instances, the family may be struggling, and by listening, the school can provide access to assistance (Young & Jean, 2018). This is another instance when a translator may be necessary and valuable. At times, it may be necessary to use an online service as it is difficult to find a translator for some dialects (The Big Word, 2017). When using a translator, ensure they are familiar with educational jargon and district policies so that they communicate the correct information (Young & Jean, 2018).

Family conferences, traditionally called a parent/teacher conference, offer a safe space for families and teachers to share information about the student (Mapp et al., 2017). When appropriate, the student can attend as well, and then this becomes a collaborative time where the group discusses the student and current progress, looks at student work, and has a chance to ask questions and make suggestions for improvement or continued success (Young & Jean, 2018). This interactive back-and-forth provides a meeting space where all members have the chance to participate in a positive way.

When an IEP, 504, or other district-based meeting is needed, it is important for the educator to come prepared and open-minded. Using a one-page student information sheet will ensure the educator is prepared to speak about the student in terms of success and struggles. The sheet may include things the student does well, things the student is just learning to do, things that the student does with support, things to work on during the year, as well as a few key accommodations made for the student (Johnson, 2017; Mapp et al., 2017). In this way, the educator is ready to discuss the student and can be an active participant who can answer questions as they come about.

Connections With and Among Families During the School Year

Deepening students' awareness of cultural and personal experiences takes time and can be accomplished through a visible classroom curriculum that includes families as support systems (Harmon, 2015). As families begin to see that diversity is valued and accepted, they will be more apt to work with the student at home to ensure that the social justice concepts from the classroom are reinforced (Teaching Tolerance, 2016). In this way, families and teachers are nourishing students' identities and family values at the same time. This two-pronged approach ensures consistency and adds "richness to the work of anti-bias and social justice education" (Teaching Tolerance, 2016, p. 16).

Family Events

There are several strategies that educators and schools can employ to encourage making connections with and among families. Family events such as potluck dinners, student showcases, game nights, or multicultural events will engender feelings of connection (Gonzalez, 2016). Fundraising for a community need or creating special events such as a "Martin Luther King, Jr. day celebration or LGBT pride event" (Teaching Tolerance, 2016, p. 16) will encourage families to work together where they might not have otherwise. When a family is in need of items, looking for support within the classroom and school first is another way to ensure a culture of family is being created. Adult education programs are another way to involve families and build common understanding (Young, Jean, & Mead, 2019). In this case, families might sign up for classes that help them with student learning issues, teach them English as a second language, inform them about identity development or family diversity, to name just a few (Gonzalez, 2016; Teaching Tolerance, 2016).

For their part, families have experiential insight on social justice issues, even if they do not perceive it to be true. Personal issues that involve their own culture, history, identity, and justice are all stories that will enhance student learning. Asking families and community members to share their stories at specific events "can provide inspiration as well as information" (Teaching Tolerance, 2016, p. 15). Equally important is allowing students to share their stories within the classroom as it builds personal identity and strengthens the bond between students and teacher. Family interviews and guest speakers can also break the ice and increase feelings of inclusion and support between families, schools, and teachers (Young, Jean, & Mead, 2019).

Tools for Successful Partnerships

There are myriad tools that may also assist in creating a classroom and school that values all students and creates equity for students. Educators can send letters home that explain what the student is learning, what to expect in the upcoming weeks, and what the parent can do to help (Mapp et al., 2017). It is vital that this communication be translated into each and every language in the classroom so that all families are able to engage with the work. Some educators may also invite family members to act as classroom volunteers. This allows family members to actively participate and help others.

Providing interactive learning activities are another valuable tool that enhances the partnership and gives the family a better understanding of the work and the educator a deeper appreciation for the family. The activity should be academically based on current learning that is ability leveled, culturally links school and home, requires the participation of at least one family member, offers clear directions, provides all materials necessary, and improves the self-esteem and independence of the student (Elm, 2017). Educators must also make the activity flexible so that all families can access it as well as giving a generous completion date (Elm, 2017).

Technology also provides a way for teachers to communicate with families and for students to complete work. Many families now have smartphones, and this tool is powerful. When a school or teacher uses an online application, it provides a format from which communication can be shared. ClassDojo (Class Twist, 2017), for example, can be translated into a multitude of languages, which means that parents can ask questions, comment on activities, and offer support, while teachers can post homework, requests, or positive notes and pictures. PowerSchool (2018) is another program that offers parents a portal to the student gradebook and, when set up to do so, individual classroom websites that can be as comprehensive or simple as the educator chooses.

In addition to using an online application for communication purposes, other programs offer at home tutoring and assignments for students. Parents are able to sit with the student, learn side-by-side, or simply oversee the work. These programs range from simply offering tutorials to actual assignments that the teacher can grade (Curriculum Associates, 2018; Khan Academy, 2018). In most cases, educators can assign work for students to complete, and they can ask parents to assist the student or complete the work together if the assignment calls for that.

Final Thoughts

Beginning in 1965 and moving forward to today, family-school partnerships have played an important part in education, yet they do not always receive the attention deserved (Klein, 2016; Paul, 2016). It is clear that family engagement is a vital piece of the educational puzzle and can be viewed through the social justice lens. Ensuring that there is equity in the process and that families are involved in the partnership takes considerable work from the school and the educator. Research has proven a positive connection between collaborative family-school partnerships and student outcomes to include higher academic success, lower rates of absenteeism, and greater graduation rates (Grant & Ray, 2016, O'Donnell & Kirker, 2014). Students who are supported by both family and school have better self-esteem, social skills, and work habits (O'Donnell & Kirker, 2014).

A variety of engagement frameworks suggest ways that educators and schools can set the stage for collaborative successes (Epstein, 1987; Epstein & Sanders, 2019; Hutchins et al., 2012; Mapp & Kuttner, 2013). Each of the frameworks requires the educator to carefully and methodically create the conditions that offer families a comfortable place to talk, share, and participate in the schooling of their student. Beyond the frameworks, there are specific strategies and tools that can be used to further the connections between teacher and family, while providing a two-way collaborative partnership.

Points to Remember

- *Family-school partnerships are required by federal law. Any school that receives public dollars must offer specific strategies and activities to increase collaboration between families and schools.*
- *Epstein's (2019) Six Keys to Collaboration and Mapp and Kutttner's (2013) Dual Capacity Building Framework both attempt to increase family engagement. Regardless of the framework, schools and educators are tasked with finding and understanding the challenges that exist, then creating policies and programs to encourage collaboration and, in turn,*

produce the conditions to improve both student and family outcomes.
- Social justice requires educators to consider how to provide equitable experiences and partnerships that will increase engagement and collaboration with families and students who, at first, may not feel comfortable in the classroom. It may be necessary to begin with a phone call or home visit.
- To increase communication and academic activities, educators can use programs that translate messages, share the gradebook and website, and offer academic assignments.
- Creating family nights, fundraising activities, and special events all provide opportunities for families to come together with educators, the school, and other families to increase engagement and collaboration. When seen through a social justice lens, these activities provide a chance for more equitable outcomes.

References

Castro, M., Exposito-Casas, E., Lopez-Martin, E., Lizasoain, L., Navarro-Asencio, E., & Gaviria, J.L. (2015). *Parental involvement on student academic achievement: A meta-analysis.* Retrieved from https://www.sciencedirect.com/science/article/pii/S1747938X15000032

Centers for Disease Control and Prevention. (n.d.). *Parent engagement in schools.* Retrieved from https://www.cdc.gov/healthyyouth/protective/parent_engagement.htm

Class Twist. (2017). *ClassDojo.* Retrieved from https://www.classdojo.com/resources/

Curriculum Associates. (2018). *What we do.* Retrieved from https://www.curriculumassociates.com/Solutions

Dunifon, R.E. (2018). *You've always been there for me: Understanding the lives of grandchildren raised by grandparents.* Chicago, IL: Rutgers University Press

Elm, G. (2017). *Replacing traditional homework packets with activity-based homework backpacks that require parent involvement in the early grades.* Retrieved from http://csusm-dspace.calstate.edu/bitstream/handle/10211.3/198536/ElmGretchen_Fall2017.pdf?sequence=3

Epstein, J. L. (1987). *Toward a theory of family-school connections: Teacher practices and parent involvement across the school years.* In K. Hurrelmann, F. Kaufmann, and F. Losel (Eds.), *Social Intervention: Potential and constraints,* 121-136. New York: de Gruyter.

Epstein, J. & Sanders, M.G. (2019). *School, family, and community partnerships: Your handbook for action* (4th ed.). Thousand Oaks, CA: Corwin

Flamboyan Foundation. (2011). *Setting the stage: The family engagement field.* Retrieved from http://flamboyanfoundation.org/wp/wp-content/uploads/2011/06/Setting-the-stage-4-28-11.pdf

Gonzalez, J. (2016). *A collection of resources for teaching social justice.* Retrieved from https://www.cultofpedagogy.com/social-justice-resources/

Grant, K.B. & Ray, J.A. (2016). *Home, school, and community collaboration* (3rd ed.). Thousand Oaks, CA: SAGE

Harmon, J. (2015). Social justice: A whole-school approach. *Edutopia.* Retrieved from https://www.edutopia.org/blog/social-justice-whole-school-approach-jeanine-harmon

Harvard Family Research Project. (2014*). Redefining family engagement for student success.* Retrieved from http://www.hfrp.org/redefining-family-engagement-for-student-success

Hutchins, D.J., Greenfield, M.D., Epstein, J.L., Sanders, M.G., & Galindo, C.L. (2012). *Multicultural partnerships involve all families.* New York, NY: Taylor & Francis

Johnson, B. (2017). *How to make IEP meetings more effective.* Retrieved from https://www.edutopia.org/blog/how-make-iep-meetings-more-effective-ben-johnson

Khan Academy. (2018). *About.* Retrieved from https://www.khanacademy.org/about

Klein, A. (2016). *The Every Student Succeeds Act: An ESSA overview.* Retrieved from https://www.edweek.org/ew/issues/every-student-succeeds-act/index.html

Mapp, K.L., Carver, I, & Lander, J. (2017). *Powerful partnerships: A teacher's guide to engaging families for student success.* New York: NY: Scholastic

Mapp, K. L. & Kuttner, P. J. (2013). *Partners in education: A dual capacity-building framework for family-school partnerships.* Retrieved from http://www.ed.gov/parent-and-family-engagement

McQuiggan, M. & Megra, M. (2017). *Parent and Family Involvement in Education: Results from the national household education surveys program of 2016.* Retrieved from https://nces.ed.gov/pubs2017/2017102.pdf

O'Donnell, J., & Kirker, S. L. (2014). The impact of a collaborative family involvement program: Latino families and children's educational preferences. *School and Community Journal, 24*(1), 211-234.

Parent Teacher Home Visit. (2016). *PTHV model.* Retrieved from http://www.pthvp.org/what-we-do/pthv-model/

Paul, C. A. (2016). Elementary and Secondary Education Act of 1965. *Social Welfare History Project.* Retrieved from https://socialwelfare.library.vcu.edu/programs/education/elementary-and-secondary-education-act-of-1965/

PowerSchool. (2018). *Solutions.* Retrieved from https://www.powerschool.com/

Teaching Tolerance. (2016). Critical practices for anti-bias education. Retrieved from https://www.tolerance.org/sites/default/files/2017-06/PDA%20Critical%20Practices_0.pdf

The Annie E. Casey Foundation. (2012). *Stepping up for kids: What government and communities should do to support kinship families.* Retrieved from https://www.aecf.org/m/resourcedoc/AECF-SteppingUpForKids-2012.pdf

TheBigWord. (2017). *OnDemand translations.* Retrieved from https://en-us.thebigword.com/solutions/translation

Young, N.D. & Jean, E. (2018). Penciling in parents: Making time for partnerships that count. In N.D. Young, E. Jean, & T.A. Citro, *From Head to Heart: High quality teaching practices in the spotlight,* pp. 107-120. Wilmington, DE: Vernon Press

Young, N.D., Jean, E., & Mead, A.E. (2019). *From cradle to classroom: A guide to special education for young children.* Roman & Littlefield, Lanham, MD

Chapter Three

School Law and Policy: Promoting and Protecting Diverse Students

Jennifer A. Smolinski, *American International College*

All children are entitled to the privileges associated with having a positive educational experience as a way to forge a successful life. One of the most profound cases that changed the shape of the nation's educational future was the 1954 court case of Brown vs. Board of Education (Ramsey, 2017). Here, the court ruled that to separate similarly-aged children based on race and qualifications was illegal and that a state or school that received federal funding for education was obligated to provide services and learning to everyone on equal terms (A&E Network, 2018).

After this landmark decision to desegregate schools, parents of children with disabilities began legal actions against school districts for discrimination based on the schools' previous decisions to exclude and segregate children with disabilities (Camera, 2016). Brown versus the Board of education was just the beginning of a myriad of legal changes and positive outcomes that paved the way for other laws to take root in our educational future (Ramsey, 2017).

Since Brown vs. Board of Education in 1954 many laws have been put in place to protect students, particularly those with disabilities, and provide them with the support and resources they need to succeed in an educational setting (Camera, 2016). The rights of students of all races, gender identities, abilities, and educational levels to receive the same educational opportunities are inherent (Education of Individuals with Disabilities, 2004). Improving educational results for diverse individuals is an essential element of the national policy that ensures equality of opportunity, full participation, independent living, and economic self-sufficiency for all individuals (Education of Individuals with Disabilities, 2004).

The Education for All Handicapped Children Act of 1975

The Education for All Handicapped Children Act of 1975 guaranteed a free and appropriate public education (FAPE) for every child with a disability in the United States (U.S. Department of Education, 2007). Passed by Congress in 1975, this was the first special education law specifically for students with physical and mental disabilities (University of Kansas-School of Education, 2018). The law stated that public schools must provide students with disabilities the same opportunities for education as other students and that schools that received federal funds must provide one free meal a day (U.S. Department of Education, 2007).

The Education for All Handicapped Children Act ensured that special education services were available to children with disabilities (U.S. Department of Education, 2007). Under this Act, public schools were required to provide fair, appropriate services, equal access to education, and the least restrictive school environment to students (Education for All Handicapped Children Act, 1975; University of Kansas-School of Education, 2018). Not only did this legislation change the way students with disabilities experienced education, mandating that disabilities be better identified and treated, those students' families gained the ability to exercise their right to due process (University of Washington, 2017).

The Elementary and Secondary Education Act

The Elementary and Secondary Education Act (ESEA) began in 1965 and is the most far-reaching federal legislation affecting education ever passed by the United States Congress. The original intent was to combat the achievement gap between low-income, neglected and homeless families and white, higher-income families (Klein, 2016; Paul, 2016). Provisions within ESEA aim to close the gap by setting benchmarks and goals to measure the progress of students (Paul, 2016).

Federal funding for primary and secondary school education became established, and a national curriculum was set forth (Klein, 2016). ESEA also provided a national system to hold schools accountable and increase equality in education (Klein, 2016; Paul, 2016). Most importantly, Title VI of ESEA extended provisions to children with disabilities (Paul, 2016). Every five years, the bill is reauthorized and updated to reflect the needs of students.

The Every Student Succeeds Act (ESSA) is the latest iteration of ESEA and was reauthorized in 2015 as the previous act, No Child Left Behind Act (NCLB), had included prescriptive requirements that had become increasingly unworkable for schools and educators. (U.S. Department of

Education, 2015). ESSA reiterated the goal of fully preparing all students for success in college and future careers and required educators to teach all students the same academic content while maintaining high academic standards that would prepare them to succeed in college and careers (U.S. Department of Education, 2015).

Americans with Disabilities Act & Section 504 of the Rehabilitation Act of 1973

The Americans with Disabilities Act includes protection against discrimination for students with disabilities in P-12 schools as well as in postsecondary education (University of Washington, 2017a). Coupled with Section 504 of the Rehabilitation Act of 1973, the rights of individuals with disabilities in schools, programs, and activities that receive federal financial assistance from the U.S. Department of Education are protected (U.S. Department of Justice, Civil Rights Division, 1990). In part, Section 504 provides that an otherwise qualified individual with a disability shall not be excluded from the participation in, be denied the benefits of, or be subjected to discrimination based on a disability (Council for Exceptional Children, 2018).

Section 504 also requires recipients of federal funds to provide students with disabilities appropriate educational services designed to meet the individual needs of such students to the same extent as the needs of students without disabilities (Council for Exceptional Children, 2018). To fulfill this obligation, school team members, including special education educators, along with a child's parent, create a 504 plan that provides services and changes to the learning environment (Understood, 2017).

Unlike Individualized Education Plans (IEPs), there is no standard 504 plan, and the plans do not have to be a written document; however, they must include specific accommodations and supports and/or services (Center for Parent Information & Resources, 2017). Although the plans vary by state, they are generally reviewed each year with a reevaluation occurring every three years or when needed (Understood, 2017).

Individuals with Disabilities Education Act (IDEA)

The Education for All Handicapped Children Act of 1975 was renamed as the Individuals with Disabilities Education Act (IDEA) in 1990 and improved upon special education and the services available for students with disabilities (Lee, 2018). Additional amendments created in 1997 and 2004 ensured equal access to education, among other things (University of Washington, 2017b). IDEA articulated the rights of students with disabilities and the services that were required to be provided to them in elementary and secondary school; thus, schools became more inclusive and effective in educating students with disabilities (University of Washington, 2017b). IDEA guaranteed that a student's education would be tailored to meet individual needs and delivered in the least restrictive environment (LRE) with students being placed in typical education settings with non-disabled peers when feasible (American Psychological Association, n.d.; Lee, 2018).

The same high academic achievement standards, clear performance goals, and the opportunity to achieve them must be consistent between students with disabilities and their peers (Lee, 2018). In addition, IDEA required Individualized Education Plans (IEPs) for students with disabilities and amendments made in 1997 affected student participation in assessment, the review and development of IEPs, and increased the parental role in the education of their children (University of Washington, 2017b).

Protection of Racial Isolation in Schools

The United States Government Accountability Office (U.S. GAO) has substantiated that, despite best efforts, schools are still in large part segregated by race and class, and getting worse, as evidenced by the more than 20 million students of color who now attend racially and socioeconomically isolated public schools, up from under 14 million students in 2001 (Scott, 2016). The U.S. GAO has also confirmed that high-poverty, high-minority schools are under-resourced and over-disciplined, that students attending these schools are less likely to have access to advanced coursework, and they are more likely to be suspended or expelled (Scott, 2016).

The U.S. Supreme Court addressed racial isolation by validating the idea that racially diverse schools can provide incalculable educational and civic benefits by promoting cross-racial understanding, breaking down racial stereotypes, among others, and eliminating bias and prejudice (U.S. Department of Education and U.S. Department of Justice, 2018). Scholarly research has also demonstrated that learning in diverse environments improves critical thinking and problem solving and that schools that lack a diverse student body or are racially isolated, may fail to provide the full array of benefits that P-12 schools can offer (Scott, 2016; U.S. Department of Education and U.S. Department of Education, 2015). This phenomenon is evidenced by lower academic achievement, fewer effective teachers, higher teacher turnover rates, and less demanding curricular resources as compared to more racially diverse schools (U.S. Department of Education and U.S. Department of Justice, 2018).

Providing students with diverse, inclusive educational opportunities is crucial to achieving the nation's educational and civic goals and, as such, laws have been enacted to give elementary and secondary schools the ability to voluntarily consider race in furthering their compelling interests in achieving diversity and avoiding racial isolation (U.S. Department of Education and U.S. Department of Justice, 2018).

One Supreme Court case in particular, Parents Involved in Community Schools vs. Seattle School District No. 1 (Brennan Center for Justice, 2007), provided schools with some flexibility in taking proactive measures to meet these compelling interests. Schools that are concerned that their student-body composition interferes with offering an equal educational opportunity to all of their students are able to develop general race-conscious measures that do not treat each student differently solely based on a systematic, individual typing by race (Brennan Center for Justice, 2007).

School boards may bring together students of diverse backgrounds and races through other means, such as new school strategic site selection, the development of attendance zones based on neighborhood demographics, the targeted recruitment of students and faculty, and the tracking of enrollment and performance by race (U.S. Department of Education and U.S. Department of Justice, 2018). It is essential that these race conscious methods do not lead to the differential treatment of students by telling them that they are to be defined by race (U.S. Department of Education and U.S. Department of Justice, 2018).

When developing objectives and the means to achieve diversity, school districts should be able to explain how their objectives fit within their overall mission as well as consider approaches that do not rely on the race of individual students before implementing approaches that do (U.S. Department of Education and U.S. Department of Justice, 2018). Schools may employ race-neutral approaches that use criteria such as students' socioeconomic status, parental education, neighborhood socioeconomic status, and/or geography (Ellison & Pathak, 2016).

To be fair, school districts are only required to use race-neutral approaches if they are workable, meaning they will be effective in achieving the diversity that the school district seeks or to address racial isolation, or when they are not forced to sacrifice a component of their educational mission or priorities (Ellison & Pathak, 2016). If race-neutral approaches are deemed unworkable, districts may employ generalized race-based approaches that use expressly racial criteria but do not involve decision-making on the basis of any individual student's race (Ellison & Pathak, 2016).

When using an approach that relies on individual racial classifications, a school district may only consider the race of individual students if it is narrowly tailored to meet a compelling interest, closely fits their goal of achieving diversity and/or avoiding racial isolation and is used no more than necessary to meet those goals (U.S. Department of Education and U.S. Department of Justice, 2018).

Discipline Disparities

The United States Government Accountability Office's analysis of the Department of Education's national civil rights data for 2013-2014 revealed that black students, boys, and students with disabilities were disproportionately disciplined in P-12 public schools (U.S. Government Accountability Office, 2018). These disparities were found to be widespread and persisted regardless of the type of disciplinary action, level of school poverty, or type of public school attended (U.S. Government Accountability Office, 2018).

Research suggests that implicit educator bias, including stereotypes and/or unconscious associations about people, may cause them to judge student behaviors differently based on race and sex (U.S. Government Accountability Office, 2018). Discretionary discipline practices in response to student behaviors, such as disobedience and defiance, can result in particular groups of students being more harshly disciplined than others (Liiv, 2015). Research has shown that the types of offenses that black children were disciplined for were largely based on school officials' interpretations of behavior (Liiv, 2015; U.S. Government Accountability Office, 2018).

In 2014, the U.S. Department of Education's Office for Civil Rights reported that black students were suspended and expelled at three times the rate of white students (Loveless, 2017). In particular, large racial disparities in California school districts' disciplinary practices were found, and evidence showed that black students were disproportionately dealt the harshest exclusionary penalties: expulsions and out-of-school suspensions (Loveless, 2017).

Other research has found that schools that enroll a greater percentage of black students exhibit higher suspension rates for black students than schools with fewer black students (Liiv, 2015; Loveless, 2017). California schools, for example, reported that black students received 235 out-of-school suspensions and in 2015, despite an apparent decline, the suspension rate for blacks still remained higher than for other ethnic groups (Loveless, 2017).

Out-of-school suspensions can lead to low academic performance, poor attendance, and juvenile crime, pushing students into the school-to-prison pipeline (Elias, 2013). As such, restorative justice efforts, such as meetings between victims, perpetrators, and parents, have been used as an alternative to get misbehaving students to take responsibility for their behaviors and the consequences suffered by others (Gregory & Fergus, 2017).

Federal laws require school districts to administer school discipline without unlawfully discriminating against students on the basis of race, color, or national origin (U.S. Government Accountability Office, 2018). School policies and practices can sometimes result in unlawful discrimination based on race due to students who are intentionally subjected to different treatment based on race and/or if a race-neutral policy has a disproportionate and unjustified effect on a student of a particular race (U.S. Government Accountability Office, 2018).

Individual schools have discretion in determining what discipline a student receives and some schools are reverting to other disciplinary measures, such as detention, parent conferences, or a restriction of privileges to address the unwanted behavior (Collaborative for Academic, Social, and Emotional Learning [CASEL], 2018; Positive Behavioral Interventions & Supports [PBIS], 2018). School districts have also begun to implement efforts to address student behavior or reduce the use of exclusionary discipline. For instance, alternative discipline models that emphasize behavior prevention and focus on support, such as positive behavioral interventions and supports (PBIS), restorative justice practices, and social-emotional learning (SEL), are being used to address disparities for certain student groups (CASEL, 2018; PBIS, 2018). Measures such as staff training on bias, holding student listening sessions, and the regular review of data to identify disparities reduces exclusionary discipline and improves overall school climate (U.S. Government Accountability Office, 2018).

Gender Identity and Sexual Orientation

In the United States, an estimated 3.2 million youth, ages 8-18, identify as LGBTQ+ with 1.6 million of high school students identifying as LGBTQ+ and 150,000 students age 13-17 identifying as transgender (Dowd, 2018). There are several federal statutes that currently protect students by prohibiting discrimination on the basis of sex, national original, race, and religion (Dowd, 2018).

1st Amendment to the U.S. Constitution

The First Amendment of the U.S. Constitution provides, in part, that Congress shall make no law prohibiting the free exercise of religion or the freedom of speech or the right of the people to peaceably assemble (National Archives, 2018). For students, this means that in public school, they maintain their rights to free speech and have the ability to voice their opinions about LGBTQ+ issues as well as organize peaceful protests. Students also have the right to take a same-sex date to any school event and dress and express themselves to match their gender identity (National Center for Transgender Equality, 2018).

Equal Protection Clause of the 14th Amendment to the U.S. Constitution

The 14th Amendment to the Constitution states that no state shall deny any person the equal protection of the laws (National Archives, 2018). This means that all public school students have a federal right to equal protection and that schools have a duty to protect those students that identify as LGBTQ+ from harassment the same as they do for all other students (Johnson, 2017).

Title IX of the Education Amendments

Title IX states that no person shall be excluded from participation in, be denied the benefits of, or be subjected to discrimination under any education program that receives federal financial assistance on the basis of their sex (U.S. Department of Education, 2015). Title IX, therefore, protects all educational activities, except those that are sex-specific, such as sororities, and prohibits sex-based discrimination and gender-based harassment based on a student's failure to conform to stereotypical views of masculinity and femininity (National Center for Transgender Equality, 2018).

Equal Access Act

According to the Equal Access Act, it is illegal for public secondary schools that receive federal financial assistance and have limited open meetings to deny equal access to, or discriminate against, any students who would like to conduct a discussion within that limited open meeting on the basis of religious, political, philosophical, or other content of speech at that meeting (Berkley Center, 2018). For schools, this means that for any extra-curricular activities to form, they have to allow for the formation of, for example, a Gay-Straight Alliance or LGBTQ club, and may not impose special rules or restrictions on these organizations that are not imposed on other clubs (Berkley Center, 2018; National Center for Transgender Equality, 2018).

The Family Educational Rights and Privacy Act (FERPA)

The Family Educational Rights and Privacy Act (FERPA) protects the privacy of students' educational records and applies to all schools that receive federal funds (U.S. Department of Education, 2018). As such, personal information contained in student school records are protected and cannot be shared without permission from the student and/or parents, including any information on gender, transgender status, or medical history (National Center for Transgender Equality, 2018)

Anti-Discrimination and Anti-Bullying Policies

No federal laws explicitly protect students from discrimination on the basis of sexual orientation and gender identity (Dowd, 2018). Research shows that only 20 states and the District of Columbia have anti-discrimination or anti-bullying laws that explicitly protect LGBTQ+ students and that approximately 55% of LGBTQ+ youth live in states that do not have laws that explicitly protect them from discrimination based on sexual orientation or gender identity (Dowd, 2018).

Research has shown that students who attend schools with anti-bullying or anti-discrimination policies that include statements regarding sexual orientation and gender identity experience less anti-LGBTQ+ victimization than in schools without such policies (Dowd, 2018). Schools with these protective policies provide a safe and affirming environment for LGBTQ+ students to learn, interact, and feel a sense of belonging (Dwedar, 2016).

Students who attend schools that do not have policies protecting against discrimination and bullying are more at risk for absenteeism, lower GPAs, school discipline, and decreased rates of post-secondary plans (Dowd, 2018; Dwedar, 2018). Students are additionally at risk for negative health outcomes and risky behaviors, such as lower self-esteem, higher levels of depression, and increased alcohol consumption, and increased use of illicit substances (Dowd, 2018; Dwedar, 2018). The lack of policies, coupled with the failure to implement existing protections that affirm and support LGBTQ+ students, not only leaves them with a limited education and puts them at risk for physical and psychological harm, but also undermines their fundamental rights under federal law (Dwedar, 2018).

Final Thoughts

There has been a myriad of legal changes that have paved the way for the improved future of education. Acts such as The Education for All Handicapped Children Act of 1975 and the Elementary and Secondary Education Act of 1965 hold schools accountable by requiring that diverse students, including those with disabilities, must have the same educational opportunities, and equal access to those opportunities, as all other students. Section 504 of the Rehabilitation Act of 1973 explicitly states that an otherwise qualified individual with a disability shall not be excluded from participating in, benefiting from, or be the subject of discrimination on the basis of his or her disability in school, or any other setting.

Although the laws seek to treat diverse students equally, there are some situations where, despite best efforts, schools still treat students differently by virtue of race and racial segregation. Schools that are high-poverty and high-minority have been shown to be under-resourced and over-disciplined, leading to a disparity in access to advanced coursework and groups of diverse students more likely than others to be suspended or expelled.

Attaining diverse, inclusive educational opportunities for all students is crucial and, as such, schools have been granted the ability to voluntarily consider race in furthering their compelling interests in achieving diversity and avoiding racial isolation. Schools that fear they are not providing an equal educational opportunity to all of their students have the ability to develop general race-conscious measures provided they do not treat each student differently solely based on race or another protected factor.

With these laws, policies, and regulations in place, schools have become more inclusive and effective in educating all their students. Unfortunately, some students still experience discrimination based on race, color, and/or national origin. Black students and students with disabilities are disproportionately disciplined in P-12 public schools, which may be the result of educator bias, stereotyping, and unconscious associations or judgments.

While federal laws set forth obligations that school districts must follow in meeting their obligations to administer school discipline without discriminating against particular groups of students, school policies and practices can sometimes result in unlawful discrimination. Given the discretionary ability schools have in determining disciplinary practices, some schools have reverted to implementing alternative discipline models, such as positive behavioral interventions, instead of more exclusionary practices, such as expulsion.

It is clear from the United States Constitution that all students, no matter, race, religion, color, or sexual orientation, have the right to equal protection and that schools have the duty to protect all their students and ensure that they receive an equal education that will allow them to be successful and productive members of our society and its future.

Points to Remember

- *The rights of students of all races, gender identities, abilities, and educational levels to receive the same educational opportunities are inherent, and the equality of opportunity and full participation is essential in the educational field.*
- *IDEA and ESSA set forth that schools must maintain the same high academic achievement standards and expectations, clear performance goals, and the opportunity to achieve them, for all students. Educators must teach to all students equally, regardless of ability, race, sexual orientation, and national origin, among other protected factors.*
- *When relying on individual racial classifications, the race of a student may only be considered if the approach is narrowly tailored to meet a school's compelling interest, closely fits its goal of achieving diversity, and is used no more than necessary to meet the goals.*
- *Despite federal laws that prohibit exclusionary disciplinary practices, school policies and practices can result in unlawful discrimination based on race by either intentionally subjecting students to different treatment based on race and/or implementing policy that is neutral on its face but actually has a disproportionate and unjustified effect on a student of a particular race*

References

A&E Network. (2018). *Brown v. board of education*. Retrieved from https://www.history.com/topics/black-history/brown-v-board-of-education-of-topeka

American Psychological Association. (n.d.). *Individuals with Disabilities Education Act (IDEA)*. Retrieved from http://www.apa.org/about/gr/issues/disability/idea.aspx

Berkley Center. (2018). *The unintended consequences of the Equal Access Act*. Retrieved from https://berkleycenter.georgetown.edu/posts/the-unintended-consequences-of-the-equal-access-act

Brennan Center for Justice. (2007). *Parents involved in community schools v. Seattle School District No. 1*. Retrieved from https://www.brennancenter.org/legal-work/parents-involved-community-schools-v-seattle-school-district-no-1

Camera, L. (2016). *More than 60 years after Brown v. Board of Education, school segregation still exists*. Retrieved from https://www.usnews.com/news/articles/2016-05-17/after-brown-v-board-of-education-school-segregation-still-exists

Center for Parent Information & Resources. (2017). *Parent and educator resource guide to section 504*. Retrieved from https://www.parentcenterhub.org/ocr-guide-to-section504/

Collaborative for Academic, Social, and Emotional Learning [CASEL]. (2018). *What is SEL?* Retrieved from https://casel.org/what-is-sel/

Council for Exceptional Children. (2018). *Understanding the differences between IDEA and Section 504*. Retrieved from http://www.ldonline.org/article/6086/

Dowd, M. (2018). *LGBT youth experience discrimination, harassment, and bullying in school*. Retrieved from https://williamsinstitute.law.ucla.edu/press/lgbt-youth-bullying-press-release/

Dwedar, M. (2016). *Like walking through a hailstorm: Discrimination against LGBTQ youth in US schools*. Retrieved from https://www.hrw.org/report/2016/12/07/walking-through-hailstorm/discrimination-against-lgbt-youth-us-schools#

Education of Individuals with Disabilities. 20 USC § 1400. Retrieved from http://uscode.house.gov/view.xhtml?path=/prelim@title20/chapter33&edition=prelim

Elias, M. (2013). *The school-to-prison pipeline: Policies and practices that favor incarceration over education do us all a grave injustice*. Retrieved from https://www.tolerance.org/magazine/spring-2013/the-schooltoprison-pipeline

Ellison, G. & Pathak, P.A. (2016). *The efficiency of race-neutral alternatives to race-based affirmative action: Evidence from Chicago's exam schools*. Retrieved from https://economics.mit.edu/files/11955

Gregory, A. & Fergus, E. (2017). Social and emotional learning and equity in school discipline. *The Future of Children, 27*(1), 117-136. Retrieved from https://files.eric.ed.gov/fulltext/EJ1144814.pdf

Johnson, S.F. (2017). *The 14th amendment protects individual rights in public education*. Retrieved from https://www.concordlawschool.edu/blog/14th-amendment-protects-rights-education/

Klein, A. (2016). *The Every Student Succeeds Act: An ESSA overview.* Retrieved from https://www.edweek.org/ew/issues/every-student-succeeds-act/index.html

Lee, A.M. (2018). *Individuals with Disabilities Act (IDEA): What you need to know.* Retrieved from https://www.understood.org/en/school-learning/your-childs-rights/basics-about-childs-rights/individuals-with-disabilities-education-act-idea-what-you-need-to-know

Liiv, K.E. (2015). *Defiance, insubordination, and disrespect: Perceptions of power in middle school discipline.* Doctoral dissertation. Harvard Graduate School of Education. Retrieved from https://dash.harvard.edu/bitstream/handle/1/16461057/LIIV-DISSERTATION-2015.pdf?sequence=1

Loveless, T. (2017). *2017 Brown Center report on American education: Race and school suspensions.* Retrieved from https://www.brookings.edu/research/2017-brown-center-report-part-iii-race-and-school-suspensions/

National Archives. (2018). *The Constitution of the United States.* Retrieved from https://www.archives.gov/founding-docs/constitution

National Center for Transgender Equality. (2018). *Know your rights.* Retrieved from https://transequality.org/know-your-rights/schools

Paul, C. A. (2016). Elementary and Secondary Education Act of 1965. *Social Welfare History Project.* Retrieved from https://socialwelfare.library.vcu.edu/programs/education/elementary-and-secondary-education-act-of-1965/

Positive Behavioral Interventions & Supports [PBIS]. (2018). *Schoolwide PBIS for beginners.* Retrieved from https://www.pbis.org/school/swpbis-for-beginners

Ramsey, S. (2017). *The troubled history of American education after the Brown decision.* Retrieved from http://www.processhistory.org/american-education-after-brown/

Scott, B. (2016). America's schools are still segregated by race and class. That has to stop. Retrieved from https://www.theguardian.com/commentisfree/2016/may/19/america-schools-segregation-race-class-education-policy-bobby-scott

U.S. Department of Education (2007). *25 years of progress in educating children with disabilities through IDEA.* Retrieved from https://www2.ed.gov/policy/speced/leg/idea/history.html

U.S. Department of Education. (2015). *Title IX and sex discrimination.* Retrieved from https://www2.ed.gov/about/offices/list/ocr/docs/tix_dis.html

U.S. Department of Education. (2018). *Family Educational Rights and Privacy Act* (FERPA). Retrieved from https://www2.ed.gov/policy/gen/guid/fpco/ferpa/index.html

U.S. Department of Education, Office for Civil Rights. (2015). *Title IX and sex discrimination.* Retrieved from https://www2.ed.gov/about/offices/list/ocr/docs/tix_dis.html?exp=0

U.S Department of Education and U.S. Department of Justice. (2018). *Guidance on the voluntary use of race to achieve diversity and avoid racial isolation in elementary and secondary schools.* Retrieved from https://www2.ed.gov/about/offices/list/ocr/docs/guidance-ese-201111.html

U.S. Department of Justice, Civil Rights Division. (1990). *Information on technical assistance on the Americans with Disabilities Act.* Retrieved from https://www.ada.gov/ada_intro.htm

U.S. Government Accountability Office. (2018). *Discipline disparities for black students, boys, and students with disabilities.* Retrieved from https://www.gao.gov/assets/700/690828.pdf

Understood. (2017). *The difference between IEPs and 504 plans.* Retrieved from https://www.understood.org/en/school-learning/special-services/504-plan/the-difference-between-ieps-and-504-plans

University of Kansas-School of Education. (2018). *Timeline of the Individuals with Disabilities Education Act (IDEA).* Retrieved from https://educationonline.ku.edu/community/idea-timeline

University of Washington. (2017a). *What Federal U.S. legislation protects the rights of students with disabilities.* Retrieved from https://www.washington.edu/doit/what-us-federal-legislation-protects-rights-students-disabilities

University of Washington. (2017b). *What is the individuals with disabilities act?* Retrieved from http://www.washington.edu/doit/what-individuals-disabilities-education-act

Chapter Four

Gender and Sexual Orientation: Understanding the Differences Among Students

Elizabeth Jean, *Endicott College*

Doris L. Buckley, *Northern Essex Community College*

American society has come to a point where it is critical to rethink common categories of gender, sex, and sexuality (Adams & Bell, 2016). Debates and questions of gender and sexual conformity have permeated popular culture and fervor continues to increase in every aspect of society, from television to policy in workplaces and schools (Adams & Bell, 2016). In May of 2016, the U.S. Department of Education issued guidance designed to ensure that transgender students are protected from discrimination on the basis of gender identity (Kahn, 2016). It is now imperative that educators support transgender students and provide safe and inclusive school environments, regardless of one's own experience, knowledge, or comfort with transgender individuals (Kahn, 2016; Wimberly, 2015).

Beyond battles of students' rights into locker rooms and restrooms based on one's gender identity, students are still struggling for basic acceptance (Orr & Baum, 2018). High levels of bullying, harassment, and other forms of victimization continue to permeate. The bullying of sexual and gender minority youth is widespread, with documented negative impacts on overall health (Newman, Fantus, Woodford & Rweigema, 2017). Verbal and physical assault by peers and humiliation by their peers and teachers continue to be real problems in America's schools (Kahn, 2016). As such, it is important to consider the differences and similarities in gender identity and transgender youth as well as to provide a social justice framework for school leaders and educators that necessitates a welcoming space where all children, including those with gender-expansive identities, can thrive (Wimberly, 2015).

Ages and Stages of Gender Identity Development

Gender identity typically develops in stages. By around age two, children become conscious of the physical differences between boys and girls. Before age three, most children can easily label themselves as either a girl or a boy. By age four most children have a stable sense of their gender identity. During the early childhood years, children learn gender role behavior (Berk, 2017). Regardless of future gender identity, cross-gender preferences and play are a normal part of gender development and exploration.

By age six, most children spend most of their playtime with members of their own sex and may be attracted towards sports or other activities that are associated with their gender. Children typically express their gender identity through the social relationships they develop, clothing or hairstyle choices, and social behavior that reflects varying degrees of aggression, dominance, dependency, and gentleness (Berk, 2017).

Gender stereotypes have changed over time. One example of this is the fact that more and more female athletes excel at their sports. The increased number of women in science and other fields historically dominated by men is another example. Over time, society has recognized that stereotypes of masculine and feminine activities and behaviors are inaccurate and limiting to a child's development. One's ability to predict who a child is based on early preferences is not very accurate and may be harmful if it leads to shame or attempts to suppress a child's skills, talents or sense of self.

Understanding the Language

Learning appropriate language in relating to the transgender community is an important first step for educators to help students feel safe and supported (Kahn, 2016). Gender diverse is a general and encompassing term used to describe a range of labels that individuals may utilize when their gender identity, expression or perception does not conform to the norms and stereotypes others expect (Rafferty, 2018b). Gender identity refers to an individual's internal sense of who they are, based on an interplay between environment, developmental factors, and biological traits (Rafferty, 2018b). This may be male, female, somewhere in between, a combination of both or neither (Rafferty, 2018b). Gender expression refers to the way a person presents their gender identity externally such as through clothing, hairstyle, or behavior (Kahn, 2016). Gender expression may be masculine, feminine or androgynous (Kahn, 2016).

When a baby is born, there is a proclamation of whether or not the baby is a boy or a girl, male or female. This proclamation of sex is based on physical attributes and is referred to as biological sex or sex assigned at birth (Orr & Baum, 2018). For most individuals, this declaration will align with their gender identity. Cisgender is the term used to describe individuals in this category (Orr & Baum, 2018; Kahn, 2016). Transgender refers to individuals whose assigned sex at birth does not align with one's gender identity. The term transgender is an adjective. Using the term as a verb or a noun is offensive and should be avoided (Orr & Baum, 2018).

With the emergence of puberty, individuals realize their sexual orientation, or whom they may fall in love with. This sexual identity is referred to as sexual orientation (American Psychological Association [APA], 2013; Kahn, 2016). Lesbian, gay, bisexual, and straight are all examples of sexual orientations (Orr & Baum, 2018). It is not uncommon for adolescents to struggle during this period as they make sense of their attractions versus what they feel is expected in their familial and social settings. Like gender identity, an individual's emotional and physical attraction to a member of the opposite or same sex cannot be changed and is very difficult to predict in early childhood (Rafferty, 2018b). Some adolescents may experience immediate acceptance and understanding of their sexual orientation, while others have families that have a more difficult time navigating their child's gender identity, thoughts, and feelings. Just as in the stages of grief, some parents find themselves going through similar stages of shock, denial, anger, bargaining, and acceptance (Rafferty, 2018b).

Transition is the process through which an individual begins to live as the gender with which they identify, rather than the one typically associated with their sex assigned at birth. Social transition may include changing clothing and hairstyle as well as changing their name and preferred pronouns. Medical transition includes medical components such as gender therapy and gender-affirming surgeries (Orr & Baum, 2018).

Gender Dysphoria

Gender dysphoria has been defined as unhappiness with an individual's given gender (Yarhouse, 2016). It is a general term, not the same as gender nonconformity, which refers to behaviors not matching the gender norms or stereotypes of the gender assigned at birth (Rafferty, 2018c). Gender nonconformity examples include girls dressing in ways more socially expected of boys or cross-dressing in adult men. Gender dysphoria is also not the same as being gay/lesbian (Rafferty, 2018c).

The Diagnostic and Statistical Manual of Psychiatric Disorders, often referred to as the DSM-5, provides a diagnosis of gender dysmorphia (APA, 2013). It is, therefore, important to distinguish experiences of gender dysphoria with the diagnosis of Gender Dysphoria (capitalized for the sake of clarity). The diagnosis of Gender Dysphoria states that "unhappiness with an individual's given gender has risen to the level of an enduring, significant cross-gender identification and personal distress or impairment in important areas of functioning such as work or school" (APA, 2013). It can be diagnosed in children, adolescents, or adults with symptoms of incongruence between one's experiences or expressed gender and assigned gender being felt for a minimum of six months in duration (APA, 2013).

Gender Dysphoria diagnosis in children involves the presence of six or more of the following paired with significant impairment or distress for at least six months (APA, 2013):

1. A strong desire to be of the other gender or an insistence that the individual is the other gender.
2. A strong preference for wearing clothes typical of the opposite gender.
3. A strong preference for cross-gender roles in make-believe play or fantasy play.
4. A strong preference for the toys, games or activities stereotypically used or engaged in by the other gender.
5. A strong preference for playmates of the other gender.
6. A strong rejection of toys, games, and activities typical of an individual's assigned gender.
7. A strong dislike of an individual's sexual anatomy.
8. A strong desire for the physical sex characteristics that match an individual's experienced gender.

Children begin showing gendered interests and behaviors between the ages of two and four (Rafferty, 2018a). Gender atypical behavior is common among young children and may be part of normal development. Children who meet the criteria for gender dysphoria may or may not continue to experience it into adolescence and adulthood (Rafferty, 2018c).

In adolescents and adults, gender dysphoria diagnosis involves a difference between an individual's experienced/expressed gender and assigned gender, and significant distress or problems functioning. It lasts at least six months and is shown by at least two of the following (APA, 2013):

1. A marked incongruence between an individual's experienced / expressed gender and primary and / or secondary sex characteristics.
2. A strong desire to be rid of primary and / or secondary sex characteristics.
3. A strong desire for the primary and / or secondary sex characteristics of the other gender.
4. A strong desire to be of the other gender.
5. A strong desire to be treated as the other gender.
6. A strong conviction that the individual has the typical feelings and reactions of the other gender.

The Social Transition

A social transition for transgender students is the process of presenting as a member of the opposite gender in different contexts such as preferred clothing or pronouns used to reference the self (Durwood, McLaughlin & Olson, 2017). In a research study completed by Durwood et al. (2017), regarding the well-being of socially transitioned children, it was found that reported depression and self-worth of transgender children did not differ from their matched control group or sibling peers. Transgender children showed typical rates of depression compared with national averages (Durwood et al., 2017). Children reported just slightly higher levels of anxiety while parents' report of anxiety in their children were higher than in the control group (Durwood et al., 2017).

The findings from this study suggest that children who have socially transitioned are less likely to suffer the impact of high levels of depression and anxiety often found with gender-nonconforming children who had not socially transitioned (Durwood et al., 2017). This research also lessens concerns that parents of socially transitioned children could be underreporting mental health concerns (Durwood et al., 2017).

Practical Considerations for Schools

The Gay, Lesbian and Straight Education Network (GLSEN) published its most recent National School Climate Survey in 2016 on the experience of gender diverse students and included over 10,500 students between the ages of 13 and 21, from all 50 states, as well as the District of Columbia

(Kosciw, Greytak, Giga, Villenas & Danischewski, 2016). This report, along with other literature refers to the community of gender diverse individuals as LGBTQ, a widely accepted initialism for lesbian, gay, bisexual, transgender, and the q referring to "queer" or "questioning". The survey consistently indicated that gender diverse students continue to face a myriad of challenges in school. Eight out of ten LGBTQ students (81.6%) reported that their school engaged in LGBTQ-related discriminatory policies or practices, with two-thirds (66.2%) saying that they personally experienced this anti-LGBTQ discrimination (Kosciw et al., 2016).

As a result of hearing anti-LGBTQ language and experiencing victimization and discrimination, many LGBTQ students avoid school activities or miss school entirely (Kosciw et al., 2016). Specific school-based supports are related to a safer and more inclusive school climate, including: supportive educators, LGBTQ-inclusive curriculum, comprehensive anti-bullying policies, and supportive student clubs, such as Gay-Straight Alliances (Kosciw et al., 2016).

First impressions matter when welcoming all students into a classroom that will become a community of learners. Black and Almango (2018) offer some suggestions for cultivating a classroom environment that is tolerant of differences and where all students may thrive. For older students, course syllabi may include the teacher's name and preferred pronouns (she, her hers; he, him, his; or they, them, theirs) to show the way in which gender is expressed. This is done not necessarily for the teacher's sake. It is a way of letting students know that there is an awareness and comfort with discussions of gender identity. Other suggestions include allowing students to introduce themselves whenever feasible (Black & Almango, 2018). Teachers set the tone by introducing themselves with their name and pronouns and including what they would like to be called in the classroom setting; therefore, students are encouraged to follow suit. Teachers can then address students by their preferred name and pronouns and also use preferences in class discussions (Black & Almango, 2018). These suggestions help to build a classroom environment of trust and tolerance for all students.

Children's awareness and understanding of being transgender may emerge at any time during the P-12 years since gender identity is typically established around age 4 (Rafferty, 2018a). Including an awareness of transgender students is important for elementary, middle, and high schools. Transgendered students are often misgendered by others, often unintentionally but sometimes with intent to cause harm (Smith, Frey, Pumpian & Fisher, 2017).

Educators should reflect upon their own assumptions regarding gender identity. These assumptions may include preferred activities for boys and girls. After developing an understanding of personal beliefs and biases and understanding the appropriate language that should be used when referencing students, the educator can then take a proactive role and speak up as a model of inclusive behavior (Kahn, 2016; Orr & Baum, 2018).

Creating a safe space for students begins with modeling the expectation for civil behavior for all students and staff. Stepping in when derogatory or hurtful language is used is sometimes necessary. It is not always known which students may be struggling with their gender identity. A safe and nurturing classroom and school environment will help to ensure the success of all students, regardless of gender identity (Kahn, 2016; Orr & Baum, 2018).

The entire school community must be committed to creating a school environment that is inclusive and supportive for transgender students. School leaders should provide professional development for all staff on transgender inclusion. Some of the most successful trainings involve students or parents of transgender students who have had to navigate challenging situations in the school environment and will be able to offer suggestions of ways in which a school can do better (Kahn, 2016; Orr & Baum, 2018). Teaching with social justice in mind is a continual process of evaluation for school leaders. It is more than just a series of trainings but the cultivation of a climate that is welcoming and conducive to learning for all students, regardless of race, ethnicity, or gender identity.

Religious-based, homophobic discourse must be acknowledged. It permeates religious institutions such as places of worship and faith-based schools as well as secular microsystems such as public schools and families across society and structures (Newman et al., 2017). The language and ideology of personal religious beliefs are often cited as a rationale for bullying behaviors and may also serve as a rationale for nonintervention by teachers, administrators, school staff and family members. An integrated approach to diversity and social justice in schools involves recognizing the ways in which personal views on a variety of topics impact the understanding of oppression against those with nonconforming gender identities or expressions (Adams & Bell, 2016). Exploring topics such as civil rights laws, employment discrimination, and relationship violence all assist in framing one's experiences and offer opportunities to build bridges of understanding between individuals and groups (Adams & Bell, 2016).

Students must learn to respect one another. A lack of respect can be displayed in many ways and can affect a wide range of students. Teachers who display respectable behavior and acceptance towards all students teach their students to do the same (Smith et al., 2017). Every educator comes to the classroom with his or her own set of beliefs, past experiences, and viewpoints that need to be addressed on a personal level. Equity-conscious educators spend time in self-reflection, acknowledging mistakes that may have been made in the past and planning for classroom practices that will better promote social justice. The integration of literature that includes transgender characters is one way that educators can promote positive discussions between students and educators (Smith et al., 2017). The use of appropriate pronouns, as previously mentioned, is another way of modeling respect and an openness to diverse gender identities for students.

Privacy and disclosure concerns should be anticipated when creating an inclusive school environment for transgender students. Each individual's transition and circumstances will be unique. Some children will arrive at school with a gender identity already established. For others, especially those individuals growing up in a particular community, the transition may be more public. Safeguards should be established to ensure that a student's and family's choices are honored in the school setting as well as by school personnel outside of school (Orr & Baum, 2018).

Choice of bathroom and locker room use is an important consideration when creating school policies. Negative mental health consequences have been found among transgender youth and adults who have been denied access to public facilities based on their gender including increased stress, fear, and suicidality (Seelman, 2016; Weinhardt, Stevens & Xie, 2017). Children and youth should have access to all programs and spaces based on gender identity (National Center for Transgender Equality, 2018). This includes restrooms, locker rooms, athletics, overnight field trips, and homecoming court and prom (National Center for Transgender Equality, 2018). Misconceptions abound about potential threats to safety and other inappropriate behaviors (Seelman, 2016; Weinhardt, Stevens & Xie, 2017). Schools must have expectations for appropriate behavior and policies that ensure the safety of all students, regardless of gender identity (National Center for Transgender Equality, 2018).

Most schools have anti-bullying policies in place. These policies are critical for transgender and gender-expansive students. Schools should be equity-conscious, ensuring that students feel respected for who they are. Careful attention must be given to bullying prevention and addressing harassment when it occurs (Smith et al., 2017). Documented evidence indicates that gender-expansive youth regularly experience discrimination and harassment because of their sexual orientation and gender identity

(Dowd, 2018). LGBTQ youth continually feel unsafe in schools with over a fourth being physically harassed because of their gender identity or sexual orientation (Dowd, 2018). Any incident of discrimination, harassment, or violence must be thoroughly investigated, corrective action must be taken, and both students and staff should have access to appropriate resources. Complaints of discrimination or harassment based on an individual's actual or perceived transgender status or expression should be handled in the same way as any other discrimination or harassment complaint (Orr & Baum, 2018).

School counselors provide a key role in addressing the marginalization of transgender students in schools. By partnering with school administrators to offer professional development on transgender and gender nonconforming students, educators can learn helpful approaches and ways to provide a welcoming classroom environment, contributing to a positive school culture towards all learners (Mason, Springer & Pugliese, 2017).

There is a need for sexual and gender minority youth (SGMY) to receive opportunities for interpersonal connection, fostering a sense of belonging, and to receive accurate information about sexuality and gender to help facilitate positive identity development (Steinke, Root-Bowman, Estabrook & Levine, 2017). These opportunities will help to counteract the discrimination and negative mental health impact many SGMY experience and help them access needed supports (Steinke et al., 2017).

Final Thoughts

It is important to understand that oppression against nonconforming sexual and gender identified individuals is rooted in misogyny and patriarchy (Adams & Bell, 2016). Misogyny is the hatred or dislike of women and values or concepts associated with females (Adams & Bell, 2016). Patriarchy is a social system in which men are the primary authority figures, occupying roles of political leadership, moral authority, and control of property. In the patriarchal belief system, female-identified behaviors and attributes are either not valued or only valued for their position under the subordination of men (Adams & Bell, 2016).

Both misogyny and patriarchy continue to be barriers to not only the rights of women but are especially challenging to overcome in creating a society that supports transgender and gender-expansive individuals (Adams & Bell, 2016). Schools provide an important place to challenge stereotypes and help to create a more just society. With an understanding of transgender and gender-expansive students, as well as policies and practices that support all students, today's schools can provide places where children and youth can pursue interests, talents and intellectual pursuits that will contribute to society.

Points to Remember

- *The use of appropriate language in relating to the transgender community is an important first step in helping students feel safe and supported and provides a positive example for students and other staff members to follow.*
- *First impressions matter in creating a classroom space that is inclusive and supportive of transgender students.*
- *Privacy and disclosure concerns should be anticipated with safeguards in place to ensure a student's and family's choices are honored in the school setting as well as by school personnel outside of school.*
- *Anti-bullying policies should be in place in all schools. Complaints of discrimination or harassment based on an individual's actual or perceived transgender status or expression should be handled in the same way as any other discrimination or harassment complaint.*
- *Educational leaders must model respectful and inclusive behaviors that students can be expected to follow. This will allow for the success of all learners in today's schools.*

References

Adams, M., Bell, L., Goodman, D., & Joshi, K. (2016). *Teaching for diversity and social justice.* New York, NY: Routledge.

American Psychiatric Association. (2013). *Diagnostic and statistical manual of mental disorders* (5th ed.). Washington, DC: APA

Berk, L.E. (2017). *Child Development.* Saddle River, N.J.: Pearson Education.

Black, A. & Almango, S. (2018). Contemporary advice from a transgender student. Faculty Focus: *Higher Education Teaching & Learning.* Magna Publications. Retrieved from: https://www.facultyfocus.com/articles/effective-classroom-management/contemporary-classroom-advice-from-a-transgender-student/.

Dowd, M. (2018). *LGBT youth experience discrimination, harassment, and bullying in school.* Retrieved from https://williamsinstitute.law.ucla.edu/press/lgbt-youth-bullying-press-release/

Durwood, L., McLaughlin, K. & Olson, K. (2017). Mental health and self-worth in socially transitioned transgender youth. *Journal of the American Academy of Child & Adolescent Psychiatry, 56*(2), 116-123. DOI: 10.1016/j.jaac.2016.10.016

Kahn, E. (2016). The schools transgender students need. *Educational Leadership, 74*(3), 70-73. Retrieved from: http://www.ascd.org/publications/educational-leadership/nov16/vol74/num03/The-Schools-Transgender-Students-Need.aspx

Kosciw, J., Greytak, E., Giga, N., Villenas, C. & Danischewski, D. (2016). *The 2015 National School Climate Survey: The experiences of lesbian, gay, bisexual, transgender, and queer youth in our nation's schools.* New York: GLSEN.

Mason, E., Springer, S. & Pugliese, A. (2017). Staff development as a school climate intervention to support transgender and gender nonconforming students: An integrated research partnership model for school counselors and counselor educators. *Journal of LGBT Issues in Counseling, 11*(4), 301-308. DOI: 10.1080/15538605.2017.1380552

National Center for Transgender Equality. (2018). *Know your rights.* Retrieved from https://transequality.org/know-your-rights/schools

Newman, P.A., Fantus, S., Woodford, M.R., & Rweigema, M. (2017). "Pray that God will change you": The religious social ecology of bias-based bullying targeting sexual and gender minority youth-A qualitative study of service providers and educators. *Journal of Adolescent Research, 33*(5), 523-538. DOI: 10.1177/0743558417712013

Orr, A. & Baum, J. (2018). Schools in transition: A guide for supporting transgender students in K-12 schools. *Human Rights Campaign.* Retrieved from https://www.hrc.org/resources/schools-in-transition-a-guide-for-supporting-transgender-students-in-k-12-s

Rafferty, J. (2018a). Gender identity development in children. *American Academy of Pediatrics.* Retrieved from https://www.healthychildren.org/English/ages-stages/gradeschool/Pages/Gender-Identity-and-Gender-Confusion-In-Children.aspx

Rafferty, J. (2018b). Gender-diverse & transgender children. *American Academy of Pediatrics.* Retrieved from https://www.healthychildren.org/English/ages-stages/gradeschool/Pages/Gender-Diverse-Transgender-Children.aspx

Rafferty, J. (2018c). Ensuring comprehensive care and support for transgender and gender-diverse children and adolescents. *American Academy of Pediatrics.* Retrieved from http://pediatrics.aappublications.org/content/142/4/e20182162.

Seelman, K. (2016) Transgender Adults' Access to college bathrooms and housing and the relationship to suicidality, *Journal of Homosexuality, 63*(10), 1378-1399. DOI: 10.1080/00918369.2016.1157998

Smith, D., Frey, N., Pumpian, I., & Fisher, D. (2017). *Building equity: Policies and practices to empower all learners.* Alexandria, VA: ASCD.

Steinke, J., Root-Bowman, M., Estabrook, S. & Levine, D. (2017). Meeting the needs of sexual and gender minority youth: Formative research on potential digital health interventions. *Journal of Adolescent Health, 60*(5), 541-548. DOI: 10.1016/j.jadohealth.2016.11.023

Weinhardt, L., Stevens, P. & Xie, H. (2017). Transgender and gender nonconforming youths' public facilities use and psychological well-being: A mixed-methods study. *Transgender Health, 2*(1), 140-150. DOI: 10.1089/trgh.2017.0020

Wimberly, G. (2015*). LGBTQ Issues in education: Advancing a research agenda.* Washington, D.C. American Educational Research Association.

Yarhouse, M. (2015). *Understanding gender dysphoria: Navigating transgender issues in a changing culture.* Downers Grove, IL: IVP Academic.

Chapter Five

Reaching and Teaching Adoptees in the Classroom: Making All Feel Welcome

Karen Russo, *St. Joseph's College, New York*

The word "diversity" brings to mind various images related to race, gender, age, culture, and ability. Teachers strive to make everyone feel loved and welcomed by considering all the ways in which students are unique. To encourage community within our classrooms, teachers have become somewhat expert in imagining ways to celebrate students' families, stories, interests, and talents. In all that they do, educators strive for inclusiveness.

In spite of teachers' best efforts, there are children in their classrooms who don't feel accepted. They are carrying the weight of a story that is their own but is rarely told by them. Some don't quite know what to make of it yet. Some are not ready to share. They fear the reactions of others. They often do not have the answers others seek. They walk a line between nature and nurture. They were…adopted.

Historical Overview of Adoption in the U.S.

Adoption, as a concept, is as old as humankind. The United States has a rich history of adoption, though not all of it is flattering. Unwed mothers, in particular, were often pressured to surrender their babies for fear that the child would bring shame to her and her family (Siegel & Smith, 2012). Social and financial constraints made it unlikely that an unwed mother would be able to parent her child. Until the mid-nineteenth century, "illegitimate" children were identified as genetically inferior to those born to married couples. Adoption records were often sealed, closed, and anonymous making it impossible for adoptees to pursue their families of origin. The secrecy around adoption was thought to benefit birthparents, adoptive parents and the adoptee. Many adoptees were never even told of their adoption. They overheard a whisper or discovered a paperwork trail that revealed the truth about how they came to be part of their families.

In 1851, Massachusetts passed the first formal law, the Adoption of Children Act (Herman, 2011; The Encyclopedia Britannica, 2018). It directed judges, for the first time, to ensure that adoption decrees were "proper" (Herman, 2011). This was the first legal step that considered the child's interests. Despite the movement toward appropriate and legal adoption practices, thousands of children were still being placed without a formal process (The Encyclopedia Britannica, 2018). Between 1854 and 1929 a quarter million orphaned and homeless children were transported from coastal cities to the Midwest on "Orphan Trains" to rural families seeking children to raise on their farms (Brown, 2011). Upon children's arrival, prospective parents merely looked at the crowd and selected the children they wanted (Brown, 2011). Children provided labor in exchange for rearing, and many were stigmatized in their new towns for years to come.

Thankfully, there has been a shift in attitudes and procedures regarding adoption in the modern day with the inclusion of more open adoptions (Vandivere, Malm, & Radel, 2009). Siegel and Smith (2012) report findings from a survey of 100 U.S. adoption agencies indicating that 95% now offer open adoptions as an option. Birthparents may choose to stay present in the child's life to varying degrees over time and contact between them can be fully disclosed by the parties or mediated by an agency (Siegel & Smith, 2012).

The increased access to media, especially social media, has made it possible for celebrities and other notable people to publicly share their adoption journeys, yet many adults choose not to adopt (Newman, 2008). Most people are raising children who are biologically linked to them, whether they be birth parents or extended birth family members. Eventually, children who were adopted become aware of this reality (Neil, 2012). They may not know the historical context of adoption. To them, it matters very little how the norms have changed. They are not ready to synthesize the complexities of the issue. They just feel different. They are not sure of their place in the world. They do not feel like their parents' "real" child. Some may even feel like they are imposters in their own lives. They fantasize about a life that could have been if circumstances were different. They are not sure who they are.

U.S. Adoption in the Modern Day

There is a strong culture of adoption in the United States. Experts estimate that 100 million Americans have been personally touched by adoption or know someone who was or has adopted (Chapman, 2017). The National Council for Adoption (NCFA) has conducted 7 national surveys periodically since 1982 with the latest survey, conducted in 2014, confirming that 110,373 domestic adoptions occurred that year (Jones & Placek, 2017). Of those, 41,023 were related adoptions (at least one adoptive parent is related by birth or marriage to one of the birthparents) and 69,350 were unrelated adoptions (adoptive parent has no relation to either birth parent biologically or through marriage) (Jones & Placek, 2017). Though international adoption has been steadily decreasing since 2004, the Department of State reported 5,647 international adoptions in 2015 with China, Ethiopia, and Ukraine topping the list of adoptees' country of origin (Jones & Placek, 2017).

The U.S. Department of Health and Human Services Administration for Children and Families (2017) reported that 437,465 children were placed in the foster care system in 2016. The sheer number of children who are not being raised in biological nuclear families may be surprising to some. It demands that educators and parents alike find ways in which adoptees and their families can be welcomed and included in all aspects of schooling.

Adoptees in School

Teachers may not be aware that a particular child in the class was adopted or is in the process of being adopted (i.e. a child in foster care), as it usually depends on how much parents and children are willing to disclose (Zill & Wilcox, 2018). Transracial placements can sometimes be indicators, but certainly not always. In all cases, a family's privacy should be respected. All children, and adopted children in particular, own their story. They should not feel obligated to discuss their families unless they initiate the discussion. Adoptive parents may choose to share information with teachers in order to provide context or insight related to the child's needs (Zill & Wilcox, 2018).

In a typical educator preparation program or professional development setting, teachers are not prepared to discuss adoption in the classroom. Their knowledge is based on previous personal contact and exposure from the media (Schoettle & Singer, 2016). Unfortunately, the majority of media coverage of adoption is negative and stigmatizing and broadcast news stories, especially, portray adoptees as fundamentally different (Kline, Karel, & Chatterjee, 2006). They often depict adoptive familial relationships as problematic or depict adoptees as having undesirable attributes (Kline et al., 2006). Not all media coverage is equal, however, and international adoption stories changed according to adoptees' country of origin (Jacobson, 2014). Reports on adoptions from Russia were more likely negative, whereas adoptions from China were more likely to be positive (Jacobson, 2014). This kind of media bias is problematic for adoptees and their families. Lack of preservice (or in-service) teacher preparation, coupled with media influence, often leads to teachers' uncertainty about what to say when the topic of adoption arises; thus, an opportunity for teachers to offer support to adopted students is lost. Adoptees may interpret the silence as disapproval (Schoettle & Singer, 2006).

Adoption is not a "one size fits all" construct. This presents further challenges for the professional development of teachers. There is diversity within the adoption community, including infant, international, older child, cross-racial, sibling groups, or kinship adoptees. Teachers must be taught how to "provide a sensitive and tolerant environment in which adoption and various family configurations are positively reflected in the classroom" (Mitchell, 2010. p. 1).

Some adoptees, particularly those who were adopted internationally, may require services based on linguistic or emotional needs. Knowledge of these needs will inform teaching practices and methods so that they thrive in their new environment (Baker, 2012). In addition to academic and developmental needs, adoptees might benefit from support in the social sphere. Palacios, Moreno, and Román (2013) found that international adoptees have a higher "visibility" than their peers. This could be due to differences in physical traits, a tendency toward friendliness, or being known as adoptees and therefore, perceived as different (Palacios et al., 2013). This visibility is not always welcomed by the adoptees, and they may struggle with feeling that they are on display (Palacios et al., 2013).

Though international adoptees have some protective factors against bullying (higher socioeconomic status and competent parents), they are vulnerable due to differences in physical characteristics such as skin tone or other features. In one Finnish study, nearly 20% of international adoptees ages 9-15 reported such experiences at least two to three times a month (Raaska et al., 2012). By providing comprehensive and appropriate education, teachers can support achievement, eliminate bias, reduce stereotypes, and raise expectations for international adoptees (Gay, 2002).

Teachers should also consider students' emotional well-being in school. All adopted children have experienced the loss of their birthparents, even if that loss cannot be recalled from infancy (Fineran, 2012). Some have survived abuse and neglect, while others may have spent years in orphanages or in foster care (Mitchell, 2010). Adopted stepchildren are similar to children with two adopted parents in that they experience feelings of separation and loss (Stewart, 2010). Blended and stepfamilies have become so commonplace in modern day schools that this population often gets excluded from consideration in the adoption realm.

School psychologists and guidance counselors should be called upon to work with adoptees on feelings of grief when they arise. These feelings may be triggered by a lesson, a thought, a situation at home, or when faced with tough questions from others. Questions may be asked by curious persons or by bullies. Barratt (2011) states that adoptees are often confronted with questions they cannot answer or perhaps with ones they don't know how to answer. By third or fourth grade, adoptees are not likely to share information with their parents about how adoption is discussed at school, and this causes a breakdown in parent-teacher communications (Schoettle & Singer, 2016). Adoptees may not seek help for themselves without parental intervention; thus, it is important for teachers to maintain awareness of such peer-interactions and look for changes in behavior, attitude, or mood.

Early life trauma can result in adoptees' difficulty in forming and sustaining relationships (Dann, 2011). Children with disrupted attachment in the early stages of life may struggle to adapt in school; they may be anxious, and/or have a negative self-image (Webber, 2017). An educator's misperceptions about adoption being a happy ending for students may discount the fact that finding a permanent family does not erase the impact of that trauma; thus, these students may not be on the teacher's "radar" (Gore Langton, 2017).

Feeling accepted in all areas of life is an important part of a child's development, so it is no surprise that students long for the acceptance of others at school. Adoptees need to know where they can go to gain a sense of belonging; yet, many do not have the information necessary to feel a true sense of identity (Mahmood & Visser, 2015). Their identity development includes questions about their birth family and the circumstances surrounding their adoption, and it may also be linked to school, social class, and peer groups. Barratt (2011) suggested that teachers help adoptees manage friendships and focus on school requirements, in order to strengthen their bonds with others and to help all children see commonalities rather than differences. Nowak-Fabrykowsi's (2014) study suggested that teachers (1) looked for the strengths in each child, (2) refrained from making assumptions about children and their families, (3) got to know as much as possible about each student's background, and (4) kept open communication between home and school.

The Portrayal of Adoptees in Classroom Books

Stories about adoptees can be found throughout history. In folklore and fiction, adoptees are sometimes heralded as champions, leaders, and role models who have overcome the adversity of their humble beginnings. Other stories portray orphans as scheming street urchins, using their grit to survive without parental guidance on the streets. Mattix and Crawford (2011) explored a plethora of adoption picture books and found that four general themes were evidenced in this subset of children's literature to include "the precious child, the search for identity, the pursuit of adoption, and the sense of belonging" (p. 313). Whether positive or negative, accounts such as these shape personal attitudes and feelings toward adoption.

In stocking the classroom library and presenting reading material to the class, teachers should select books of all genres that convey positive messages about adoption, including biographies of well-known persons who were adopted. Cultural icons such as Maya Angelou, Steve Jobs, Marilyn Monroe, and John Lennon were adopted, as were former presidents and first ladies Gerald Ford, Bill Clinton, Nancy Reagan and Eleanor Roosevelt (Show Hope, 2014). Athletes Lance Armstrong, Scott Hamilton, and Babe Ruth were adopted, as were fictional characters Annie, Superman, Spiderman, Anne of Green Gables (Show Hope, 2014). Biblical accounts of the lives of Moses, Esther, and Jesus make reference to their adoptions as well (Show Hope, 2014).

Class Assignments and Projects

Classroom assignments and projects have the potential to be problematic; thus, they must be adapted to suit the needs of all students (Mitchell, 2007). Offering a completely different assignment for adopted and foster children than the rest of the class further isolates them from the norm as they may be the only ones submitting the alternative project. This can highlight their work in ways that are not productive. By developing adaptations beforehand, no one is the wiser. It is truly inclusive before it is even presented to the students.

Autobiography. A typical autobiography begins by telling the facts (names, dates, places, circumstances) surrounding the person's beginning. That is, the day of birth. This can be incredibly difficult for an adoptee as some simply do not know the details of that day, while others find it too painful to share. It is important that children know how an autobiography is written and how it reads. This can be accomplished by exposing them to many well-written accounts as opposed to asking students to write one themselves (Mitchell, 2007). If narrative writing is the goal, perhaps focusing on a special day in the student's life might work instead.

Baby pictures. Asking adoptees to provide baby pictures can cause unnecessary stress if photos are unavailable or if sharing them is undesirable. As an alternative, ask students to provide photos of their younger selves (at any age previous to the current day) for special projects and class activities (Mitchell, 2007).

Family tree. Many adoptees do not know the names of birth family members, yet they might simply want to include the phrase "birthmother" or "birthfather" in their family tree project. Standard family tree templates do nothing to acknowledge the presence of a birth family. Allowing students to represent their families in a circle, a web, or a rooted tree are all fine choices (Mitchell, 2007). In addition, children should be encouraged to include all types of caring people (close friends, clergy, caseworkers, teachers, etc.) into a "family" project.

Heritage or ancestry projects. These assignments are often referred to as "cultural" projects, when in fact they are nothing of the sort. Culture is defined as "the customary beliefs, social forms, and material traits of a racial, religious, or social group" (Merriam-Webster, 2018, n.p.). It is not transmitted by genetic means. So, a child born in South Korea who was then adopted by German-American parents would have no connection to South Korean culture. German culture? Maybe. American culture? Yes.

When teachers assign these kinds of projects, it is with the best intentions, that is to highlight and celebrate diversity. Generally, this means students are expected to research their country of origin and report on its geography, history, and language. They might be asked to come to school in customary attire or bring traditional foods to share. Refer back to the example of the South Korean-born adoptee. Does the student share food from South Korea? Germany? The United States? Think about the child whose heritage is not known. What does the student present to the class? The situation can be avoided if teachers instead assign projects based on family customs, traditions, and celebrations rather than those connected to ancestral origins (Mitchell, 2007). Keeping this assignment in the present, as opposed to the past, can make adoptees contributions more meaningful.

Student of the week/month. Adoption is not inherently related to a student of the week/month honor, except for the autobiographical narrative and/or photos that may accompany them. One way to avoid this is to ask students to describe their interests or hobbies instead of a prescribed "all about me" paragraph (Mitchell, 2007).

Special events. As children move through their schooling years, they are undoubtedly faced with events intended for one particular parent (mother-daughter teas, father-daughter dances, and the like) or even mother's/father's/grandparent's day. To avoid a negative impact on adoptees (and frankly, any child who is growing up in a non-traditional household), events should be planned to include any special person in the child's life (Mitchell, 2007). Teachers should allow adoptees to share as much or as little of their stories as they want, this might include their homecoming day or their adoption day.

Fundraisers and special projects. Fundraisers often include language of adoption that is confusing to some, especially the adoptee. Examples such as 'Adopt an Acre of Rainforest', 'Adopt-A-Highway', and 'Adopt a Penguin' could instead be framed with language such as 'sponsor', 'support' or 'aid' as this shift will facilitate inclusiveness (Mitchell, 2007).

The impact of using positive adoption language cannot be stressed enough. Teachers should avoid using outdated language to describe adoptive families. Children were not 'given up' for adoption, rather they were 'placed' or their birthparents 'made an adoption plan' for them. Biological parents should be named as such (or as birthparents), rather than 'real parents' (Mitchell, 2010). While teachers may not be aware of modern, inclusive, and respectful terms, guidance is readily available. Through credible sources on the web, in other print, through support organizations, and through the families themselves, teachers can educate themselves on the most appropriate ways of using adoption-related terms in the presence of students and elsewhere.

Final Thoughts

There is much that can be done for teachers to inform them and illuminate the challenges adoptees face in the school setting and in society at large. Though the optimal solution would be ongoing professional development and close working relationships with families and adoption experts, teachers need not rely on outside help to improve the educational and social experiences of adoptees. Teachers can greatly enhance classroom experiences for all children by altering assignments, carefully selecting readings, and using positive adoption language. Children who were adopted, those in foster care, or those being looked after by adults other than their birthparents are at times feeling unnatural, isolated, and misunderstood. Teachers can practice compassion and inclusion in the truest sense when steps are taken to respond to their needs.

Points to Remember

- *Though the U.S. has a rich history of adoption, the effects of secrecy, shame, and negative media portrayals leave teachers wondering if and how they should address adoptees' needs.*
- *The sheer numbers of adoptees demand that teachers offer academic, social, emotional, and curricular support to students who are being raised outside of their biological families.*
- *Books, assignments, and projects should be altered to increase sensitivity and understanding of adoptees' challenges related to self-image and identity.*
- *Professional development of preservice and in-service teachers is preferred; however, teachers can gather information through their own pursuits of inclusive literature, strategies, and positive adoption language.*
- *Fully inclusive classrooms reinforce the dignity and worth of each and every child within it regardless of personal histories.*

Resources

Suggested Titles for Pre-School Learners

Adopted Like Me by Jeffrey LaCure

Adoption by Fred Rogers

Adoption Stories for Young Children by Randall B. Hicks

Beginnings: How Families Come to Be by Virginia Kroll

I Am Adopted by Norma Jean Sass

My Real Family by Emily Arnold McCully

Story of Adoption: Why Do I Look Different by Darla Lowe

Twice Upon a Time: Born and Adopted by Eleanor Patterson

We Belong Together by Todd Parr

A Mother for Choco by Keiko Kasza

Suggested Titles for Elementary Learners

A Forever Family by Roslyn Banish

Adoption by Judith Greenberg

Adoption Is For Always by Linda Walvoord Girard

Being Adopted by Maxine B. Rosenberg

Did My First Mother Love Me? by Kathryn Ann Miller

Families Are Different by Nina Pellegrini

How Babies and Families Are Made by Patricia Schaffer

How I Was Adopted by Joanna Cole

Mario's Big Question: Where Do I Belong? by Carolyn Nystrom

The Mulberry Bird: A Story of Adoption by Ann Braff Brodinsky

Real Sisters by Susan Wright

We Are Family by Sandra D. Lawrence

References

Baker, F. S. (2013). Making the quiet population of internationally adopted children heard through well-informed teacher preparation. *Early Child Development and Care, 183*(2), 223-246. DOI:10.1080/03004430.2012.669757

Barratt, S. (2011). Adopted children and education: The experiences of a specialist CAMHS team. *Clinical Child Psychology and Psychiatry, 17,* 141–150.

Brown, A. (2011). Orphan trains (1854-1929). *Social Welfare History Project.* Retrieved from http://socialwelfare.library.vcu.edu/people/mott-lucretia-coffin

Chapman, D. (2017). *As foster care adoptions increase, so does the number of waiting children.* Retrieved from https://adoption.com/study-finds-foster-care-adoptions-have-increased

Dann, R. (2011). Look out! "Looked after"! Look here! Supporting "looked after" and adopted children in the primary classroom. *Education 3-13, 39*(5), 455-465. DOI:10.1080/03004279.2010.488069

Fineran, K.R. (2012). Helping foster and adopted children to grieve the loss of birthparents: A case study example. *The Family Journal: Counseling and Therapy for Couples and Families, 20*(4), 369-375. DOI: 10.1117/1066480712451230

Gay, G. (2002). Preparing for culturally responsive teaching. *Journal of Teacher Education, 53*(2), 106-116. DOI:10.1177/0022487102053002003

Gore Langton, E. (2017). Adopted and permanently placed children in education: From rainbows to reality. *Educational Psychology in Practice, 33*(1), 16-30. DOI:10.1080/02667363.2016.1217401

Herman, E. (2011). Adoption history in brief. *VCU Libraries: Social Welfare History Project.* Retrieved from https://socialwelfare.library.vcu.edu/programs/child-welfarechild-labor/adoption/

Jacobson, H. (2014). Framing adoption: The media and parental decision making. *Journal of Family Issues,* 35(5), 654. Retrieved from https://ez.sjcny.edu/login?url=https://ez.sjcny.edu:2099/docview/1502037161?accountid=28722

Jones, J. & Placek, P. (2017). *Adoption by the numbers: A comprehensive report of U.S. adoption statistics.* Retrieved from National Council for Adoption website: http://www.adoptioncouncil.org/files/large/249e5e967173624

Kline, S. L., Karel, A. I., & Chatterjee, K. (2006). Covering adoption: General depictions in broadcast news. *Family Relations,* 55(4), 487-498. Retrieved from https://ez.sjcny.edu/login?url=https://ez.sjcny.edu:2099/docview/213933671?accountid=28722

Mahmood, S., & Visser, J. (2015). Adopted children: A question of identity. *Support for Learning,* 30(3), 268-285. doi:10.1111/1467-9604.12095

Mattix, A. A., & Crawford, P. A. (2011). Connecting the dots: Exploring themes in adoption picture books. *Early Childhood Education Journal,* 39(5), 313-321. DOI:10.1007/s10643-011-0475-8

Merriam-Webster. (2018). *Culture.* Retrieved from https://www.merriam-webster.com/dictionary/culture

Mitchell, C. (2010). *Back to school: A guide to making schools and school assignments more adoption-friendly* (Adoption Advocate Issue No. 27). Retrieved from National Council for Adoption website: http://www.adoptioncouncil.org/images/stories/NCFA_ADOPTION_ADVOCATE_NO27.pdf

Mitchell, C. (2007). *Adoption awareness in school assignments A guide for parents and educators* [Pamphlet]. Amherst, NY: Tapestry Books. Retrieved from http://www.adoptionpolicy.org/Adoption_Awareness_Schools.pdf

Neil E. (2012). Making sense of adoption: Integration and differentiation from the perspective of adopted children in middle childhood. *Children and Youth Services Review,* 34(2), 409-416. DOI: 10.1016/j.childyouth.2011.11.011

Newman, S. (2008). *Why more people don't adopt.* Retrieved from https://www.psychologytoday.com/us/blog/singletons/200810/why-more-people-don-t-adopt

Nowak-Fabrykowski, K. (2015). Nurturing development of foster and adopted children. *Early Child Development and Care,* 185(3), 486-495. DOI:10.1080/03004430.2014.936430

Palacios, J., Moreno, C., & Roman, M. (2013). Social competence in internationally adopted and institutionalized children. *Early Childhood Research Quarterly,* 28(2), 357-365. Retrieved from DOI: 10.1016/j.ecresq.2012.08.003

Raaska, H., Lapinleimu, H., Sinkkonen, J., Salmivalli, C., Matomaki, J., Makipaa, S., & Elovainio, M. (2012). Experiences of school bullying among internationally adopted children: Results from the Finnish adoption (FINANDO) study. *Child Psychiatry and Human Development, 43*(4), 592-611. DOI:10.1007/s10578-012-0286-1

The Editors of Encyclopedia Britannica. (2018). *Adoption*. Retrieved from https://www.britannica.com/topic/adoption-kinship#ref793718

Schoettle, M. & Singer, E. (2016). *Adoption at school* (C.A.S.E. Fact Sheet Series No. 9). Retrieved from http://adoptionsupport.org/wp-content/uploads/2016/05/09-Adoption-at-School.pdf

Show Hope. (2014). *30 famous people who were adopted*. Retrieved from https://showhope.org/2014/03/10/30-famous-people-adopted/

Siegel, D.H. & Smith, S.L. (2012). *Openness in adoption from secrecy and stigma to knowledge and connections*. Retrieved from http://www.adoptioninstitute.org/old/publications/2012_03_OpennessInAdoption.pdf

Stewart, S. D. (2010). The characteristics and well-being of adopted stepchildren. *Family Relations, 59*(5), 558-571. Retrieved from https://ez.sjcny.edu/login?url=https://ez.sjcny.edu:2099/docview/815402809?accountid=28722

U.S. Department of Health and Human Services, Administration for Children and Families, Administration on Children, Youth and Families, Children's Bureau. (2017). The AFCARS Report (No. 24). Retrieved from https://www.acf.hhs.gov/cb

Vandivere, S., Malm, K., & Radel, L. (2009). Adoption USA: A chartbook based on the 2007 National Survey of Adoptive Parents. Washington, DC: The U.S Department of Health and Human Services, Office of the Assistant Secretary for Planning and Evaluation. Retrieved from https://www.ncbi.nlm.nih.gov/pmc/articles/PMC4789094/#R45

Webber, L. (2017). A school's journey in creating a relational environment which supports attachment and emotional security. *Emotional & Behavioural Difficulties, 22*(4), 317-331. doi:10.1080/13632752.2017.1295553

Zill, N. & Wilcox, W.B. (2018). *The adoptive difference: New evidence on how adopted children perform in school*. Retrieved from https://ifstudies.org/blog/the-adoptive-difference-new-evidence-on-how-adopted-children-perform-in-school

Chapter Six

Racial, Ethnic, and Linguistic Diversity: Meeting Students Where They Are

Charles B. Hutchison, *The University of North Carolina at Charlotte*

Jonimay Morgan, *The University of North Carolina at Charlotte*

Michelle Pass, *The University of North Carolina at Charlotte*

The U.S. Census Bureau projects that by 2050, almost two-thirds of all American children will be students of color (U.S. Census Bureau, 2017). Juxtaposed to this is the fact that over 80% of teachers are white, monolingual women many of whom have had little direct or authentic experiences with children from communities of color and/or may have been socialized to uncritically accept negative stereotypes and deficit views of students of color (Landsman & Lewis, 2012). The changing dynamics of the nation's schools has resulted in a widening cultural and racial mismatch between students and teachers, providing a compelling rationale for a more nuanced understanding of the interactions between white teachers and students of color, specifically, students' non-dominant cultural capital.

To be a successful teacher in a non-white classroom requires the recognition of students' non-dominant culture and how to pedagogically engage with it (Ladson-Billings, 2009; Milner, 2011). Dominant culture is viewed as the system of mainstream and widely accepted social practices and ideas, often based on the ways of life of social groups with the most power in our society (Zirkel & Johnson, 2016). Members of the dominant culture, therefore, are primarily white Americans, whereas people of color are largely not members of the dominant culture. When teachers are not equipped to understand and manage intercultural gaps and challenges, cultural conflicts arise in the classroom, resulting in compromised teaching and learning processes.

The fact that most P-12 educators in the United States do not share their students' racial, ethnic, or linguistic backgrounds is an important factor in understanding teachers' attitudes and beliefs about students of color. This disparity reflects and reinforces teachers' deficit view of students of color—a view that is granted legitimacy through claims of colorblindness and the idealized notion (mostly among people of privilege) that the United States operates under a purely meritocratic system of equal opportunity for all who possess the so-called 'right' values, attitudes, and work ethic (Hinton, 2015).

In the practical sense, Pollack (2013) researched the ways in which 'teacher talk' correlated to perceptions of students of color. The study found that teachers believed the educational and economic disparities that students of color experienced were individual, not structural deficiencies, such as a culture of poverty, lack of positive role models, poor parenting, lack of value for education, loss of family values, and language deficiencies (Pollack, 2013). Deficit-based teacher talk demonstrates a lack of understanding and appreciation of the cultural capital and funds of knowledge brought into the classroom by students of color (Pollack, 2013). The resulting feelings of misunderstanding, alienation, and disrespect by students and families of color contribute to the widening of the cultural divide.

Seeking to understand the connection between teacher expectancy outcomes and teacher perceptions of future trajectories, Dabach, Suárez-Orozco, Hernandez, and Brooks (2018) highlighted the fact that teachers attributed their students' futures to family-related explanations more often than to structural factors. These deficit explanations blamed the trajectories of students of color on external loci, such as the students' home lacking valuable cultural factors (Dabach et al., 2018). The researchers also found that the teachers expected the trajectories of students of color to lead to restaurant and retail work, manual labor, unemployment, childbearing and rearing, and technical trades, even though the students were only in elementary and middle school at the time of the study (Dabach et al., 2018). Teachers' explanations of students' success or failure can affect their motivations to help students, as well as have negative developmental implications, whether directly or indirectly communicated (Bertrand & Marsh, 2015).

Cultural Capitalism and Teaching and Learning

Before there can be a discussion of cultural capital and its significance in education, it is essential to first briefly examine what is meant by culture as it pertains to current dialogue. Although culture by definition is dynamic, with no set definition, in the context of education it is one that is frequently used and is therefore crucial to understand. In relation to education, culture refers to sets of ideas, beliefs, and acquired knowledge that are passed on through teaching and learning— both consciously and unconsciously (Goldenberg, 2014). The way an individual talks, acts, and thinks are all reflections of cultural upbringing. Since schools are often seen as integral sites for cultural transmission, reproduction, and socialization, these beliefs, attitudes, and behaviors have the potential to significantly impact the relations and communication between students and teachers in diverse schools (Goldenberg, 2014). While culture is often generalized to a group of people, it is not synonymous with race and may be shaped by a variety of factors, such as social class, language, religion, and immigration status (Goldenberg, 2014).

Cultural capital is a concept that was conceived by Bourdieu (1977) to broadly define cultural identifiers, such as mannerisms, dress, beliefs, values, and artistic preferences, that have societal value and increase social mobility. Bourdieu (1977) theorized that students of color and low-economic status did not possess, by happenstance of cultural upbringing, the ability to accrue the cultural capital of the dominant white culture favored in educational systems. The disproportionate majority of white teachers often experience a cultural mismatch, rendering teaching and learning ineffective. It has been argued, however, that discussing cultural capital through such a framework views students of color through a lens of deficiency, as if their own cultural capital brought into the classroom is lesser than that of the dominant white society (Rodriguez, 2013; Yosso, 2005; Zipin, Sellar, & Gates, 2015). It is important, therefore, to examine the cognitive assets (or the funds of knowledge) students of all backgrounds—including those with low cultural capital—bring to the classroom, and how such assets impact teaching and learning.

Funds of Knowledge and Schooling

Before addressing the funds of knowledge of students of color, however, it is instructive to be reminded that the teaching force lacks diversity, with a teaching force comprised of mostly white, middle-class women (Milner, 2010). In schools that serve low-income areas especially, it may be argued that many teachers of color themselves, having been largely educated in Euro-centric environments of contexts, may find themselves as interlopers in schools that are predominantly populated by students of color. In a sense, it is necessary to distinguish teachers who are 'of the community' from those who are 'from the community', and it is obvious that this distinction can be rather complex. Although one might hurriedly conclude that a teacher from the same community is preferable to one of the community, one may risk the proposition that the latter could sometimes be preferable. The rationale is that the teacher who is 'of the community' understands and remembers personal experiences such as financial challenges, and therefore tries to implement learning activities and policies that foster learning for low-income student populations (for example, by not asking for students to pay fees for a bus trip or not to buy expensive supplies for school work) is arguably a more effective instructor. On the other hand, a teacher 'from the community' who, having been educated outside of the community mindset and has forgotten her origins, has the potential to fail in a school that serves people similar in early experiences.

Considering the scarcity of teachers of color in the teaching force, Moll (2015) refers to teaching in the United States as a commuter profession with most teachers living in communities other than those of their students. Teachers as commuters is not an issue of logistics but is representative of the larger sociocultural disconnect between P-12 teachers and their students (Moll, 2015). Ultimately, there is often a cultural incongruity between students and their teachers—both along racial and socio-economic lines.

When there is a cultural mismatch between students and teachers, it is imperative that teachers develop the skills necessary to engage students from diverse backgrounds and develop pedagogical strategies that acknowledge and encompass the cultures of their students (Ladson-Billings, 2009). If this is not done effectively, the result may be the so-called achievement gap between white students and students of color in P-12 public schools (Milner, 2010). Closing the achievement gap has been the focus of substantial educational reform efforts; however, educational reform efforts have failed to acknowledge that the educational deficits encountered by most students of color are not solely the result of limited resources but encompass other disparities that limit opportunities for students of color to receive an equitable education (Ladson-Billings, 2006; Milner, 2010).

One such disparity is the disproportionate ratio of white teachers to non-white students and the resulting lack of culturally responsive pedagogical strategies utilized by these educators. Goldenberg (2014) refers to this dynamic as a racial mismatch; however, it is not limited to race, but also includes cultures. Cultural differences can lead to cultural conflicts within the classroom when teachers ignore the "skills, interests, and knowledge" (Goldenberg, 2014, p. 112) of their students and teach strictly from a white, Eurocentric perspective. Individuals "interpret behaviors, information, and situations through our own cultural lenses; these lenses operate involuntarily, below the conscious awareness, making it seem our own view is simply the way it is" (Delpit, 2006, p.151). Teaching from this perspective, without regard to students' culture, is dismissive and devalues the culture of students of color, which can cause students to be resistant to schooling, but not to the idea of academic achievement (Carter, 2006). Students of color may perceive school as a place that is unwelcoming and where their cultural capital is discounted (Goldenberg, 2014).

To engage students in the process of teaching and learning, white teachers must critically reflect on, and acknowledge, their positionality in the dominant culture and recognize their students' positionality in the non-dominant culture (Landsman & Lewis, 2006). Teachers must assign value to the cultures of students of color by incorporating diverse cultures, not just their own Eurocentric culture, in their pedagogical practices. If white teachers are to understand and incorporate the cultures of the diverse student population in their pedagogical practices, then white teachers must make the classroom a space where students can openly express their unique backgrounds and lived experiences. Positive student-teacher interactions are crucial to student success (Goldberg, 2014).

In the practical sense, Gay (2013) emphasized the benefits of teaching to cultural diversity and the importance of connecting "in-school learning to out of school living" (Gay, 2013, p. 49). Teaching about racially and ethnically diverse groups from merely a historical perspective, as is the case in conventional education, provides students with only a partial description of a racial or ethnic group. This type of teaching can serve as a foundation on which to build a more comprehensive depiction of the "lives, cultures, contributions, challenges, and experiences" (Gay, 2013, p. 49) of that group as is the intent of culturally responsive teaching.

Culturally responsive teaching creates a sense of community within the classroom with students bringing their varied forms of cultural capital into the classroom (Goldenberg, 2014). One such form of cultural capital is linguistic capital, which refers to students' ability to speak two or more languages and to serve as translators for their families (Yosso, 2005). Lee (2017) acknowledges African American Vernacular English (AAVE) as a form of linguistic capital that is not viewed as proper English; yet, should be valued as a form of self-expression by African American students. Howard (2001) writes that students of color are more expressive and impulsive in their actions, while white students are more systematic and restrained. Teachers must come to accept that the ways students engage in the classroom are reflective of their culture and their lived experiences. This is the broad basis for the conceptualization of funds of knowledge.

Funds of Knowledge in Diverse Instructional Contexts

The concept of funds of knowledge was developed in the late 1980s as a form of education reform for public schools in the Southwestern United States with large Mexican student populations (Rodriguez, 2013). Its theoretical framework (and its extremities) challenges the deficit thinking prevalent in education—the notion that low school performance among students of color is caused by underlying linguistic, economic, and cultural limitations (Reyes, Iddings & Feller, 2016). Specifically, this concept sought to address the deficit thinking in education by acknowledging the cultural practices of students of color and their families as a form of social capital (Reyes et al., 2016). Funds of knowledge, then, are the historically accumulated bodies of knowledge and skills essential for household functioning and well-being (Gonzalez, Andrade, Civil, & Moll, 2001). By capitalizing on, and valuing, the wide variety of skills, knowledge, and competencies forged in the everyday lives and community histories of students of color, classroom instruction can be organized to increase quality and effectiveness of their learning experience (Gonzalez et al., 2001). An example of this might be when teachers visited the homes of their students of Mexican descent and witnessed activities such as gardening, construction, and open market transactions (Rodriguez, 2013). After identifying the skills and knowledge students brought to the classroom, those teachers incorporated them into educational practice. This resulted in the improved performance of those students, broke down barriers of prejudice and stereotypes that propagate deficiency narratives, and connected in school education to the out-of-school education and lifestyles of students of color (Rodriguez, 2013).

Similarly, teachers in a rural, agricultural city visited the homes of their students and created an Agriculture Field Day school event using mathematics, writing, and reading lessons that related to agriculture and connected the students' everyday lives to their classroom activities (McIntyre, Swazy, & Greer, 2001). In this way, teachers created a learning environment where students were able to utilize the funds of knowledge they brought to the classroom, as well as provided opportunities for the parents and community to participate in students' learning experiences.

In the context of teaching and learning with funds of knowledge, a study conducted by Aguirre et al. (2013) offered a practical insight as the participating teachers ultimately created lessons, 47% of which included what researchers considered meaningful connections and transitional lessons; that is to say, lessons that successfully connected observed community experiences and students' funds of knowledge, with mathematically challenging problem-solving. One example utilized in a third-grade classroom involved a teacher who began the lesson with role-playing. Students recreated a scene where they were at the grocery store having a conversation in Spanish about the grocery list with 'Abuela' (grandma). While the math instruction was conducted in English, this activity used Spanish as a classroom resource. Students were then tasked to use Abuela's shopping list to calculate the cost of items, and whether the funds provided ($40 or $70) would cover the costs. The lesson included photos and prices that the students and families were familiar with at their local Las Socias grocery store (Aguirre et al., 2013).

Another lesson from Aguirre and colleagues' study (2013) was centered around the concept of a family dinner, which required students to obtain recipes from home that they would like to share with the class. They were tasked with finding the total ingredients that would be needed for their size family. This allowed students to connect their home funds of knowledge with a math lesson. Additional tasks of the lesson required students to compare store prices and take transportation into consideration (Aguirre et al., 2013). The level of mathematical reasoning and alternate ways of completing the task was flexible, based on the students' real-world experiences. While the remaining lessons found in the study did not fully incorporate students' funds of knowledge with challenging mathematical problem-solving, they did attempt to connect familiar community knowledge and experiences to motivate traditional math assignments, such as replacing a traditional cookie-cutter shopping list with the name "pow-wow celebration shopping list" (Aguirre et al., 2013, p. 187).

A final example of funds of knowledge in lesson planning involves the use of family dialogue journals to foster connections among teachers, students, and parents. To this end, Moll (2015) believed that these journals have the potential to allow participants to establish relationships and to engage with each other through written exchanges. In this effort, all participants were asked to share personal details about themselves, their beliefs, and their experiences in their journals. Moll (2015) emphasized the importance of establishing mutual trust among participants to ensure their communications were open and honest. It was thought that these journals might provide a unique opportunity for teachers, students, and parents to assume the role of learner (Moll, 2015). This approach provided teachers with firsthand documentation in the form of written exchanges with students and their parents, which could be used to establish pedagogical practices that connected with the interests, experiences, and beliefs of the students and their families. Moll (2015) warned that there might be risks associated with journal communications, as indirect communication can sometimes lead to misunderstandings, which makes mutual trust and open communication critical to the success of this approach.

Funds of Knowledge and Pedagogical Content Knowledge

The concept of pedagogical content knowledge suggested that effective educators are expected not only to know their content subject, but also the professional skills necessary to instruct different kinds of learners, given certain considerations (Shulman, 1986). These factors have been vastly researched and extended (to the point that the ideas of multicultural education may be included as a part of this domain of knowledge). In this domain of knowledge, pedagogical content knowledge is expected to include knowledge about the nature and identity of an educator's students, for example, who they are, what they are likely to know, as well as any potential misconception regarding specific topics. Such considerations are partly contingent on the socio-cultural backgrounds of the students. For this reason, a proficient instructor is expected to have some idea regarding the funds of knowledge students bring to the classroom (Shulman, 1986).

Funds of knowledge advocates for teachers to value all their students' cultural capital as dynamic, integral, and emergent, intellectual resources in educational processes (Shulman, 1986). This is likely to improve learning outcomes as the disproportional balance of power is shifted to favor the roles and values of families, communities, and cultures, regardless of the linguistic, economic, religious, social, or cultural diversity in the classroom. The types of community cultural wealth that are brought into the classroom by students of color may include the knowledge, skills, abilities, and contacts possessed and utilized by communities of color (Yosso, 2005). Such kinds of community wealth help students to resist and survive macro and micro-forms of oppression and can be manifested in six specific types of valuable cultural capital to include aspirational capital, linguistic capital, familial capital, social capital, navigational capital, and resistant capital (Yosso, 2005). Recognizing, emphasizing, and utilizing non-dominant cultural capital in the classroom to enhance student learning creates a rich and compelling learning atmosphere for students of color (Yosso, 2005).

Professional development and teacher education must address deficit views of families of color and emphasize the remediation of families and individuals, as opposed to structural barriers, to improve student outcomes and generate a critical awareness of deficit discourse and its negative influences on teaching, learning, and school-home relations. Education occurs through teacher and student interactions and for those interactions to be beneficial, students must learn through a curriculum and pedagogy that emphasizes their skills, interest, and knowledge, their cultural capital.

Identifying cultural capital is at times an ambiguous process, but there are ways in which teachers can identify and acknowledge cultural capital such as values / interests, expressions / behavior, and language / communication (Goldenberg, 2014). The ways a student dresses (such as traditional Aztec dresses), the music they listen to (such as hip-hop and reggaeton), and hobbies (such as stepping) are a few noticeable examples of non-dominant capital that will allow educators to create effective learning environments. Seeming argumentative or interacting in apparently confrontational ways may be a manifestation of cultural capital and it may affect the way in which the student verbally engages with lessons (Goldenberg, 2014). While these behaviors and expressions seem disruptive, they are reflections of lived experiences and are just a differing way of engaging. Language and communication are extremely prevalent displays of culture. This often manifests as students speaking what is known as African-American vernacular, or bilingual students as they code-switch or act as language brokers as forms of self-expression and engagement (Spooner, 2017).

Knowing the learner is crucial for teachers, allowing them to not only understand the context of their students' lives but also connect with the community and culture in which they live. Once cultural capital is identified, using a strength-based teaching strategy is the next step (Resiliency Initiatives, 2011). A strength-based teaching strategy utilizes students' cultural capital in completing assignments such as family journals and/or digital storytelling cultural memory banking to allow learners to voice their experiences and interests. Having students read a text, asking them to share their own interpretations of the story, and then writing a short essay on how their life experiences connect to the story is just one example (Llopart & Esteban-Guitart, 2018). These teaching strategies will not only provide educational opportunities for students of color with non-dominant capital but afford the entire classroom the benefits of learning various perspectives, ways of thinking, and ways of doing things.

Indigenous heritage communities and Latinx communities often employ collaboration and group work that today's institutions value (Rogoff et al., 2017). While acknowledging and utilizing cultural capital in the classroom is a dynamic and at times challenging process, it demonstrates that going beyond students' linguistic, economic, and socio-cultural differences reveals competent individuals with knowledge and skills embedded in their cultural communities and everyday lives (Rogoff et al., 2017). Although school environments cannot ignore the challenging backgrounds of students, by acknowledging cultural capital, educators potentially avoid leaning on the deficit perspective, associating students of color with economic difficulties, deficiencies, and other negative elements.

Final Thoughts

Hutchison (2011) asserts that diversity issues have caused even the best teachers, those who "have mastered content knowledge and concepts of pedagogy...to fail in diverse school environments for which they are not prepared" (p. 20). Teaching in schools where racial, ethnic, and linguistic diversity abound can be challenging for all teachers, owing to a complexity of factors. Teachers, therefore, need to prepare themselves well in order to succeed not only as good teachers for their students but also to become successful professionals for their own life's work. In the pursuit of learning to become a successful teacher of diverse learners, there is a myriad of factors to take into consideration during instructional practices, but it all begins with understanding oneself as a teacher and also understanding who one's students are.

It has been shown that underrepresented students are likely to benefit from learning environments that utilize their cultural, linguistic, and community knowledge as classroom resources. In that regard, proficient educators—especially educators of students of color—are expected not only to learn about the sources of students' funds of knowledge, but more important, know how to use this knowledge in ways that enhance the development of intellectual skills that increase opportunities for academic success. By capitalizing on home and community knowledge and, therefore, knowing students as whole persons, classroom instruction and learning environments may be organized in ways that foster meaning-making and deeper construction of knowledge. In so doing, students will not be passive consumers of knowledge, but active participants and agents in their own education.

Points to Remember

- *There is a large disparity between the average educator, who is generally a white, monolingual middle-class woman in her 40s and the average student, who is generally a lower income individual of color, often bilingual. This often creates difficulties in teaching, understanding cultural differences, and managing classroom conflicts.*

- *Cultural capital refers to mannerisms, dress, values and beliefs, and artistic preferences that are of value in society and increase social mobility. Often, the dominant culture is more likely to value their own capital over the lower class. Open discussions can help to reduce this mismatch.*
- *'Funds of knowledge' refers to skills and knowledge that have been developed over time, both culturally and historically, to help students function in the classroom. When added to the classroom culture, funds of knowledge create a deeper and more meaningful learning experience.*
- *Using strength-based teaching strategies engages students' cultural capital and even students who are non-dominant benefit from this teaching style. In essence, the entire class becomes more aware of a variety of perspectives and ways of both thinking and doing that may be different from their own.*
- *Children from all cultures are naturally curious and are natural learners; hence, they always have something to contribute to the teaching and learning processes, when motivated. When teachers discover the natural strengths and dispositions of their students (sometimes based on their communities of origin), learning is facilitated.*

References

Aguirre, J. M., Turner, E. E., Bartell, T. G., Kalinec-Craig, C., Foote, M. Q., Roth McDuffie, A., & Drake, C. (2013). Making connections in practice: How prospective elementary teachers connect to children's mathematical thinking and community funds of knowledge in mathematics instruction. *Journal of Teacher Education,* 64(2), 178-192. DOI: 10.1177/0022487112466900

Bertrand, M., & Marsh, J. (2015). Teachers' sensemaking of data and implications for equity. *American Educational Research Journal,* 52(5), 861–893. DOI: 10.3102/0002831215599251

Bourdieu, P., & Nice, R. (1977). *Outline of a Theory of Practice* (Vol. 16). Cambridge: Cambridge University Press.

Carter, P.L. (2006). Straddling boundaries: Identity, culture, and school. *Sociology of Education,* 79(4), 304-328. DOI: 10.1177/003804070607900402

Dabach, D. B., Suárez-Orozco, C., Hernandez, S. J., & Brooks, M. D. (2018). Future perfect? Teachers' expectations and explanations of their Latino immigrant students' postsecondary futures. *Journal of Latinos and Education, 17*(1), 38-52. DOI: 10.1080/15348431.2017.1281809

Delpit, L. (2006). *Other people's children: Cultural conflict in the classroom.* New York, NY: The New Press

Gay. G. (2013). Teaching to and through cultural diversity. *Curriculum Inquiry, 43*(1), 48-70. DOI: 10.1111/curi.12002

Goldenberg, B. M. (2014). White teachers in urban classrooms: Embracing non-white students' cultural capital for better teaching and learning. *Urban Education, 49*(1), 111-144. DOI: 10.1177/0042085912472510

González, N., Andrade, R., Civil, M., & Moll, L. (2001). Bridging funds of distributed knowledge: Creating zones of practices in mathematics. *Journal of Education for Students Placed at Risk, 6*(1-2), 115-132. DOI: 10.1207/S15327671ESPR0601-2_7

Hinton, K. A. (2015). Should we use a capital framework to understand culture? Applying cultural capital to communities of color. *Equity & Excellence in Education, 48,* 299–319. DOI: 10.1080/10665684.2015.1025616

Howard, T.C. (2001). Powerful pedagogy for African American students: A case of four teachers. *Urban Education, 36*(2), 179-202. Retrieved from http://citeseerx.ist.psu.edu/viewdoc/download?doi=10.1.1.886.1011&rep=rep1&type=pdf

Hutchison, C. B. (2011). *Understanding Diverse Learners: Theory and Practice.* Acton, MA: Copley Custom Textbooks.

Ladson-Billings, G. (2009). *The dream-keepers: Successful teachers of African American children.* San Francisco, CA: Jossey-Bass.

Landsman, J., & Lewis, C. W. (Eds.). (2012). *White teachers/diverse classrooms: Creating inclusive schools, building on students' diversity, and providing true educational equity.* Stylus Publishing, LLC.

Lee, A. (2017). *Why "correcting" African American language speakers is counterproductive.* Retrieved from https://scholarworks.gvsu.edu/cgi/viewcontent.cgi?article=2162&context=lajm

Llopart, M., & Esteban-Guitart, M. (2018). Funds of knowledge in 21st century societies: Inclusive educational practices for under-represented students. A literature review. *Journal of Curriculum Studies, 50*(2), 145-161. DOI: 10.1080/00220272.2016.1247913

McIntyre, E., Swazy, R. A., & Greer, S. (2001). Classroom diversity. Connecting curriculum to students' lives. In E. McIntyre, A. Rosebery, & N. Gonzalez (eds), Classroom Diversity: Connecting Curriculum to Students' Lives, pp. 76-84. Portsmouth, NH: Heinemann.

Milner, H. R. (2010). What does teacher education have to do with teaching? Implications for diversity studies. *Journal of Teacher Education, 61*(1-2), 118-131. DOI: 10.1177/0022487109347670

Milner, H. R. (2011). Culturally relevant pedagogy in a diverse urban classroom. *Urban Review, 43*(1), 66-89. DOI: 10.1007/s11256-009-0143-0

Moll, L. C. (2015). Tapping into the "hidden" home and community resources of students. *Kappa Delta Pi Record, 51*(3), 114-117. DOI: 10.1080/00228958.2015.1056661

Pollack, T. M. (2013). Unpacking everyday "teacher talk" about students and families of color: Implications for teacher and school leader development. *Urban Education, 48*(6), 863-894. DOI: 10.1177/0042085912457789

Resiliency Initiatives. (2011). *Embracing a strength-based perspective and practice in education*. Retrieved from http://www.ayscbc.org/Strengths-Based%20School%20Culture%20and%20Practice.pdf

Reyes, I., Da Silva Iddings, A. C., & Feller, N. (2016). Building relationships with diverse students and families: A funds of knowledge perspective. *Journal of Early Childhood Literacy, 16*(1), 8-33. DOI: 10.1177/1468798415584692

Rodriguez, G. M. (2013). Power and agency in education: Exploring the pedagogical dimensions of funds of knowledge. *Review of Research in Education, 37*(1), 87–120. DOI: 10.3102/0091732X12462686

Rogoff, B., Coppens, A. D., Alcalá, L., Aceves-Azuara, I., Ruvalcaba, O., López, A., & Dayton, A. (2017). Noticing learners' strengths through cultural research. *Perspectives on Psychological Science, 12*(5), 876-888. DOI: 10.1177/1745691617718355

Shulman, L. S. (1986). Those who understand: Knowledge growth in teaching. *Educational Researcher, 15*(2), 4-31. DOI: 10.3102/0013189X015002004

Spooner, M. (2017). *Code-switching and its challenges: Perspectives on translanguaging I the EFL/ESL classroom*. Retrieved from https://digitalcommons.usu.edu/cgi/viewcontent.cgi?article=2162&context=gradreports

U.S. Census Bureau. (2017). U.S. Census Bureau, Population Estimates Program (PEP). Retrieved from https://factfinder.census.gov/faces/tableservices/jsf/pages/productview.xhtml?src=bkmk

Yosso, T. J. (2005). Whose culture has capital? A critical race theory discussion of community cultural wealth. *Race, Ethnicity, and Education, 8*(1), 69–91. DOI: 10.1080/1361332052000341006

Zipin, L., Sellar, S., Brennan, M., & Gale, T. (2015). Educating for futures in marginalized regions: A sociological framework for rethinking and researching aspirations. *Educational Philosophy and Theory, 47*(3), 227–246. DOI: 10.1080/00131857.2013.839376

Zirkel, S., & Johnson, T. (2016). Mirror, mirror on the wall: A critical examination of the conceptualization of the study of Black racial identity in education. *Educational Researcher, 45*(5), 301–311. DOI: 10.3102/0013189X16656938

Chapter Seven

Advancing the Social Standing of Students from Educationally At-Risk Populations: Students Who Learn, Look, Speak, Behave, or Believe Differently

Ellen L. Duchaine, *Texas State University*

"Inclusion, in essence, is not about satisfying the needs of a minority group of society; it is rather a right of every individual...to participate in their own education and development as a person. In addition, it is how people with special educational needs demonstrate to the world that they are part of the society. And this idea must continue to be developed." (Rusanescu, Sora, & Stoicescu, 2018, p. 124).

Any student who learns, looks, speaks, behaves, or believes differently may be at risk in many classrooms around the world. Students from low-income families, students of color, students with disabilities, students struggling to learn, students with a different social skill set, students in foster care, and students learning in an environment with a different language from their peers may be at risk. Why? Differences, particularly those differences that are new to another individual, tend to cause a sense of the unknown, a bit of fear or apprehension, and often that leads to a sense of keeping a safe distance or making fun of the person, in a teasing or mean way (Shore, 2017). This sense of fear of the unknown can be overcome when individuals are immersed in the lives of people who are different on a regular basis.

Schools provide the perfect setting for learning that different is good and, better yet, that diversity is good. Schwarz (2006) points out that, "an ecosystem with a wide and diverse array of life forms is healthier, stronger, and more enduring" (p. 1). Schwarz (2006) elaborated that the more differences there are, the better the community will be. Each of us has experienced changes in society and reveled in those changes. None of us want to live in a society where we all look alike, dress alike, and eat the same foods every day!

More Alike Than Different

Students with disabilities who receive special education services are just students. The majority of these students have the capability to learn everything their non-disabled peers learn, yet they may do it differently. The National Center for Educational Statistics (2018) reports that approximately 6.5 million youth, ages 3-21, receive special education services in public schools across the United States. This is about 13% of all public school students and is consistent with reporting since 2000 (National Center for Education Statistics, 2018). Students are identified in various disability categories to include 34% with specific learning disabilities, 20% with speech or language impairments, 14% with health impairments, and students with autism, intellectual disabilities, developmental delays, and emotional disturbances each accounted for between 5 and 9% of the student population (Young, Fain, & Citro, 2019). While these students often receive instruction in segregated classrooms, 95% spend a portion of each school day in the general education classroom, while 80% receive the majority of their education in the general education setting with various levels of instructional support (National Center for Education Statistics, 2018).

A report from the U.S. Department of Education (2017) indicated youth with intellectual and emotional disabilities are more often found in lower-performing schools, and these two groups, along with students identified with autism, frequently receive curriculum modifications, reducing the amount of content learned, and seldom prepare for college or employment, reducing their chances to successfully live as an independent adult.

These students with school-identified disabilities are now understood to be typical children with special education needs that can be met through specially designed instruction as defined in Individuals with Disabilities Education Act [IDEA] (American Psychological Association, n.d.; Lee, 2018). As we better understand individuals with disabilities, these students are now less likely to be considered special education students; rather, they are typical students who have special education needs. This difference in how educators teach students who need different instructional approaches is critical in how equity plays out in the classroom.

For the purpose of eligibility and funding, each disability is defined by a series of typical characteristics and/or areas of difficulties; however, many of the characteristics are similar (Young et al., 2019). Educators and non-disabled peers will notice differences, which are often thought of as deficits, in academic, social-emotional, communication, and physical conditions that make learning difficult (Young et al., 2019). Unfortunately, when an individual presents with a physical difference, people commonly assume they are less intelligent, and treat them this way. This generates a feeling of pity and results in reduced expectations almost automatically, without even realizing the deficit attitude toward the person (Lombardi, 2016). In addition, when children struggle to process information, communicate ineffectively, or act out behaviorally, teachers and peers may naturally react with the same deficit attitude rather than interacting with an attitude of 'ableism' and value for the individual (Lombaradi, 2016).

A disabled or struggling peer might look like any of the following:

- Students who need special education services due to any of the 13 disability categories,
- Difficulties making connections between what they have previously learned, and new information being taught,
- Longer to process responses to questions,
- Struggle to focus for long periods of time,
- Difficulty sitting still or understanding personal space, impulsivity,
- Withdrawing from others due to the anxiety of getting something wrong and/or a sense of less-than that forms over time from repeated classroom failure
(Friend & Bursuck, 2012; Heward, 2013; Vaughn & Bos, 2012).

Students who are English language learners (ELL) may enter school speaking a different language; they may look, speak, behave, or believe differently, but they too are just students who are capable of learning the same things that students who do not speak a different language learn. The National Center for Educational Statistics (2018) reports that in 2015, approximately 9.5%, or 4.8 million, public school students are English language learners. This has increased since 2000 by approximately one million students. These students are diverse and come from a wide variety of countries, cultures, and languages. Although Spanish is the most common (about 7%), there are many languages spoken by students who are ELL (National Center for Education Statistics, 2018).

Similar to students with disabilities, students who are ELL may isolate themselves as they are immersed in an environment where they are not understood. Typically, these students observe others in the classroom to figure out what is going on, and they will follow what the other students are doing, even when they do not understand the spoken word (Price & Nelson, 2014). They will work to be understood by using gestures when they communicate. As students learn the new language and feel comfortable speaking it, they are prone to make many mistakes.

How others react will make a big difference in how often they take chances practicing this new language. Speaking, or basic communication skills, comes before reading and writing, which are academic language skills (Sparks, 2016). These skills develop over a period of five or more years (Sparks, 2016). Students will, therefore, exhibit irregular patterns of success in the classroom as they experiment with speaking, reading, and writing in English. These students are working extra hard throughout each day and during each lesson as they are acquiring the English language, content-related language, and content skills and knowledge (Price & Nelson, 2014). As these students work to learn so much each day, frustration and anxiety may surface resulting in social-emotional concerns that with acceptance and effective instruction will vanish over time.

Genuine Inclusion

The inclusion of all children is not just placing children together; rather, it requires facilitating the growth and development of all children (Bricker, 1995). Yet when teachers and students are faced with diversity, inclusion isn't always an immediate thought. Educators are edging toward an inclusive mindset; however, with the demands of meeting some arbitrary level of achievement, based on high-stakes testing, separate educational settings often seem promising (Rudenstine, Schaef, & Bacallao, 2017; Walsh, 2017). A strong sense of inclusion means all students must be valued and looked upon as equals (Jean & Rotas, 2019; Rudenstine et al., 2017). Every child should be regarded as capable academically, socially, and behaviorally within the classroom, the school, the community, and society (Jean & Rotas, 2019). Not all children will learn as quickly as the child sitting next to them. But not all children grow at the same rate either!

Schools that implement inclusion systematically are the most effective in removing inequitable attitudes, while simultaneously exhibiting a welcoming community, extending the inclusive attitude into society, and increasing academic achievement for all students (Epstein & Sanders, 2019; Grant & Ray, 2016). As with other skills, the earlier an inclusive pedagogy is used to inspire critical thinking of society, the more solid the foundation for lifelong attitudes of mutual respect and worthiness of individuals with differences (Hardy & Woodcock, 2015). Hardy & Woodcock (2015) found that policy at various levels (global, state, district, school, and class) requires a critical analysis of current exclusive and inclusive policies, listening to diverse student experiences, and providing professional development in diversity awareness pedagogy.

Students from low-income families, students of color, and students with disabilities continue to struggle in school across all grade levels (Bromberg & Theokas, 2013). This struggle often includes both academic and behavioral difficulties in meeting school expectations, much of which is further exacerbated with exclusionary policies such as in/out of school suspensions and alternative classes/schools (Bromberg & Theokas, 2013). All too often in the United States, students who are African American, from low-income households, boys in general, and students with disabilities are suspended at a much higher rate than other students (Sullivan, Klingbeil, & van Nortnan, 2013). For many years, the school policy of zero tolerance resulted in exclusionary processes; however, in many school districts, this policy has been eliminated in favor of more inclusive consequences (Moreno, 2016; Richardson, 1997).

Schools prepare productive citizens by teaching and practicing the true meaning of tolerance to include acceptance and respect of all differences (Gay, 2018). When teachers and schools embrace and promote inclusion, the quality of education is improved by providing equity for all (Gay, 2018; Jean & Rotas, 2019). When some are excluded or marginalized within the school, everyone loses out because a critical aspect of their development in this global society is compromised (Gay, 2018; United Nations Educational, Scientific, and Cultural Organization, 1994). Adults demonstrating belief in all children, at all times, results in both children and other adults learning to accept differences among students (Gay, 2018; Moreno, 2016). Actions of acceptance mean intervening when intolerance is observed.

The classroom offers the perfect place for adults to empower all students through opportunity and encouragement (Jean & Rotas, 2019). Teachers are there to help children learn, but also to help students help one another through service-learning experiences, tutoring, volunteering, and other classroom activities that promote acceptance of others' talents and abilities, even while they develop those very skills and aptitudes (Jean & Rotas, 2019). Some children naturally encourage others, and they should be recognized for doing so.

The teachers make all the difference in the classroom; while cooperatively, teachers who join together make the difference in the school. With an internal commitment to being fully inclusive, teachers combine the belief that all children are equal and valuable with actions that demonstrate equality and value (Vandeyar, 2017). Students who are at-risk often present with lower ability due to the barriers of poverty, race, language differences, or disabilities (Rudenstine et al., 2017). Rather than lower expectations and focus on teaching the basics to students who have not yet shown potential, teachers need to provide educational opportunities that increase the challenge level and stimulate creative thinking (Olszewski-Kubilius & Clarenbach, 2014). This demonstrates to each child and observer the belief of equality and acceptance. The teacher, additionally, must put an emphasis on observing and monitoring interactions amongst students and within the environment, ready to make changes or add lessons to make equal access and acceptance ongoing and continuous. Being willing and able to adapt is the process that allows a classroom to be fully inclusive.

Even when children are integrated into the environment, however, taking part in similar types of activities in the classroom and on the playground does not automatically ensure interactions among children with differences (Hestenes & Carroll, 2000). Children need to gain more understanding of differences to become tolerant of them and to be comfortable interacting with others unlike themselves (Serin, 2017). Tolerance is embracing, accepting, and respecting diversity. It requires attention to differences and activities intended to promote the core of not only acceptance but of understanding and empathy of the diverse groups within schools and society (Gay, 2018; Serin, 2017).

Build Acceptance into the Classroom

Classroom teachers have the responsibility and the influence to advance the social standing of students from educationally at-risk populations. Sadly, schools have outcasts, but allowing the opportunity for outcasts to exist in our schools is unacceptable! Success happens for at-risk kids "when the school represents a community of adults who care unconditionally," (Anderson, 2017, p. 13). This begins when teachers truly believe all children are valuable and reflect on their responsibility, as it is up to the classroom teacher to express kindness and respect for the students deemed 'unlikable' by others. Classroom teachers, school staff and building administrators can easily change how at-risk students who learn, look, speak, behave, or believe differently are valued within the school and class community (Anderson, 2017; Gay, 2018).

How adults treat students who are at-risk not only makes the individual students feel more valued, it changes how the other students see those special populations (Gay, 2018). It is not surprising to know that students who observe their teachers 'liking' their peers, also 'like' their peers (Hendrikx, Mainhard, Boor-Klip, & Brekelmanns, 2017). When teachers intentionally create a climate of friendships and compatibility, every child is a member of the community and celebrated (Jean & Rotas, 2019). Teachers need to periodically evaluate the social skills observed within the class to find any deficit areas, then make plans to teach the class culturally relevant social interactions to increase their knowledge of and respect towards the countless behaviors associated with the act of communication (Gay, 2018; Rudenstine et al., 2017). Saying hello with a variety of languages, gestures, or vernacular, for example, ensures emotional safety for students whose communication skills differ from the class mainstream (Sreckovic, Schultz, Kenney, & Able, 2018).

In the classroom, teacher responsibilities go beyond a compliance-based pedagogy focusing on standardized testing and instead, educator duty includes integrating mentoring within classroom practices by providing caring relationships, having high academic, behavioral, and social expectations, and consistently reflecting an anti-deficit pedagogy in the classroom to encourage student engagement (Liou, Martinez, & Rotheram-Fuller, 2015).

Struggling students want caring relationships and higher expectations from their teachers as this type of encouragement results in increased motivation and achievement at school (Liou et al., 2015). A simple way to make this shift is using children's books about different characteristics, actions, or beliefs to teach the class about differences and the wonderful qualities each person has (Sigman, Tackett, & Azano, 2016). Without the extra expenditure of special curriculums, teachers can use children's literature to examine social justice issues by thinking beyond the superficial meaning and considering any opportunity to ask open-ended questions while reading (Hardy & Woodcock, 2015). Teachers must be vigilant in choosing books to read, avoiding those that result in a 'fix' per se, and being cautious of books that are only examples of celebrating change rather than teaching acceptance. Bateson (1994) said, "our species thinks in metaphors and learns through stories" (p. 11). After reading, educators should extend the stories into the class community, making connections with the characters through discussion or drama to allow students to consider their own circumstances, and integrating the story within the class. The use of such activities will promote genuine empathy and build a circle of support (Partridge, 2018).

Guiding students to an understanding of the purpose of education within their current surroundings and conditions leads to the motivation for learning (Gay, 2018). Motivation and respect often are accomplished when the teacher provides just enough authority that students are focused, and just enough autonomy that students are engaged (Anderson, 2017). Students learn to respect themselves, each other, and the learning environment through this guidance, encouragement, caring, and expectations from the teacher. When working with students who are at a disadvantage, teachers who understand and affirm students' identities find success in the classroom because the students feel safe (Anderson, 2017).

Being proactive is essential in warding off the likelihood of students rejecting the interactions and ideas of one another; however, another part of feeling safe is being accepting of all student comments and conversations. Attention and correction should be immediate when a student conversation takes on a negative tone or includes exclusionary comments (Gay, 2018). Teachers must stop any negativity or isolating remarks and provide validation for each student. Once some individuals begin to exclude others, the damage has already occurred, and the safe learning environment is gone.

Teaching acceptance of and value in diversity is only the first step, it is important to uphold a zero tolerance for prejudice and bullying. Despite a zero tolerance for bullying, it may still occur. When bullying occurs, teachers and administrators must intervene, encourage all students to report bullying and praise students for their courage when they report it (Menesini & Salmivalli, 2017). Confront excuses that minimize the offense (Menesini & Salmivalli, 2017). Teach the school and classroom expectations, as well as the necessary social skills for open communication and self-advocacy. In addition to teaching the skills needed to eliminate bullying and to maneuver the school and classroom, teachers and administrators must address cyber safety and social networking (Menesini & Salmivalli, 2017). It is also important from a very young age that students learn desirable and appropriate communication skills when using technology to include netiquette and what happens to posts within the social media realm.

The Classroom as a Statement of Inclusivity

When students are given the motivation, respect, and autonomy to take chances, they begin to believe in themselves and their classmates. When teachers understand and affirm students' identities, especially those at a disadvantage, the learner is able to find success in the classroom because there is an overall feeling of safety (Anderson, 2017). Educators must look beyond the student to see the need. They must talk to individual students and let them know that the adults are there to support them, teach them, and protect them. Guiding individuals to an understanding of the purpose of education within the current surroundings and conditions leads to the motivation for learning. When students are motivated, they tend to participate and complete tasks (Duchaine & Fain, 2018).

Education becomes important to individuals when they are a part of something bigger. When students feel connected to the school, they want to be in school because it has a purpose and it provides comradery, as well as builds a sense of interdependence among all members of the class (Rothrock, 2017). A common theme in a community-based pedagogy is 'we are all in this together.' This is the idea behind the action of forming cooperative groups and assigning roles for collaboration through teamwork (Gillies, 2016). The teacher can impart the concept that each student is an important part of the class by letting them know, "We depend on you. If you're not here, the class won't run as well. If you're not here the group won't run as well. Someone else will have to do your job for you" (Rothrock, 2017, p. 387).

To increase this connection, teachers can generate a sense of unity and dialogue within the classroom by creating a sense of "we-ness" among the students and dissolving the "I" with a team approach. There are many ways to unite a class. One fun way to do this is shared by Boyd, Jarmark, and Edmiston (2018) explaining how the class handshake can be a process for creating unity as it develops a common language within the class because it evolved over time as a co-creation of the students.

Teachers might consider eating lunch with students at least once a week, unifying the class, and getting to know the students on a more personal level. Attending community and school events including sporting events, extra-curricular activities such as school dances, science fair, fundraisers, and music and dance performances is another way to make connections (Young & Jean, 2018). Research suggests calling every parent the first two weeks of school to begin on a positive note and let them know you want to build a constructive relationship with a shared goal of student success (Young & Jean, 2018). Engaging in casual conversations with parents at events and in the school halls or office is another way to make a more personal connection.

Educators are tasked with breaking the stereotypical thought that being different or having a disability limits intelligence and the ability to participate in life's activities. Involving students in extracurricular activities such as educational programs that provide creative problem-solving opportunities, as well as sports, science or math clubs, music, art, and drama provide opportunities to engage with others. Students who participate in group or team activities find a sense of accomplishment, new friendships, and a more active lifestyle (Richardson, Papathomas, Smith, & Goosey-Tolfrey, 2017).

Extending the classroom into the community is another way to show respect for and acceptance of diversity. Events that bring families to the school bridge the home to school gap and build shared interest in the community (Young & Jean, 2018). This can be accomplished through a variety of activities to include a showcase of the curriculum through student accomplishments, math and literacy night, speakers, and student activities (Zacarian, & Silverstone, 2017). Inclusive activities with families are especially beneficial when scheduled early in the school year to demonstrate the desire to involve families. When individual teachers plan events for their own classes, it is helpful to extend invitations to as many members of the school faculty and staff as possible. Involve or invite the specialists (i.e., art, music, technology, and physical education teachers), counselors, translators, office workers and custodians, other classroom teachers, and administration (Rothrock, 2017). It takes time and effort to involve families that have not previously been active in school events; teachers will need to be determined and open-minded when at first an event is not well attended (Grant & Ray, 2016). Consistency and variety will be rewarded over time as families feel welcome and valued.

Inspect the Classroom to Ensure a Sense of Inclusivity

Educators should inspect books, walls, handouts, center supplies, and artifacts in the classroom. Pictures and writings should be inclusive of disabilities, ethnicities, body types and sizes, languages, race, family dynamics, physical strengths and limitations, athletic ability, talents (art, music, gaming, organization, leadership, handwriting, typing speeds), careers, and socio-economic status, as well as appearance (skin color, hair color, hair type, eye color, freckles, dimples, and health issues).

Teachers must take careful inventory of everything in the room to be certain students see others like themselves in the materials within the classroom (i.e., on worksheets, in books, on posters, and in short stories). It is also important that classroom materials include individuals who are not represented within the school itself.

The goal is to orient students to all possibilities in society, so when they experience a difference, they will be open and accepting. Families used to be represented as having a father, mother, son, daughter, and pets for a long time; however, that is no longer typical in many places. Some people still make reference to children coming from a broken home. This is a deficit attitude and leads to unproductive interactions. Educators should look at the class for representation of different families, such as single mom, single dad, living with grandparents, and two moms or two dads, as well as families that are all one race versus families that are racially blended.

Being aware of who students are matters to them; therefore, it is important for educators to really get to know the students in the class. Building inclusive classrooms with intent is the only way to make it happen. Teaching acceptance is a critical part of teaching. Teachers need to understand that acceptance is taught through the actions of the adults in the room. What materials the educator uses to fill the classroom with shows students whether or not people with differences are valued.

Scrutinizing class materials and reviewing the curriculum and lesson plans previously used for misconceptions helps to be proactive in teaching. Ensure that materials do not imply certain stereotypes, such as girls are meant to be pretty and petite, while boys are big and strong. There should be pictures of people in wheelchairs doing jobs, as well as people from all ethnicities in various careers. After scrutinizing the classroom and materials, teachers should begin to build up the appearance of the room and the class materials by adding artifacts from various cultures and emphasize the world with a huge world map, or globe. Educators do not need to get rid of all materials that show old-fashioned stereotypes; however, there must be an open discussion with students about the faultiness in what is being represented. This can be done in a very positive way; for example, if a story represents a bank manager as a man, the teacher could ask the students if the bank manager could instead be a woman, someone in a wheelchair, or someone who uses hearing aids. The teacher should allow the discussion to extend to all types of differences.

Celebrating diversity is also a must and teachers should recognize individual students in the class. Educators and students alike should investigate the topics of diversity before the year begins and during the year. Lessons can teach students that people are 'more alike than different' through celebrations that highlight differences and similarities, understanding and acceptance. Teaching acceptance of self as well as others is important as many children grow up not liking the way they look, learn, etc. When teaching students how to get along and enjoy working and learning side-by-side, time will need to be spent on self-regulation of appropriate thoughts and behaviors towards others. Understanding self-regulation is more than teaching social skills; it is using critical thinking and kindness to benefit society. Educators must be ready to deal with rejection when it is heard in the classroom. This may include developing a process to replace rejection with acceptance, posting positive quotes and motivational statements, and using pictures, books, artifacts, world maps, art, and posters. Creating activities that include sharing and cooperation, as well as teaching words from the students' home languages, demonstrating traditions, and sharing the differences in daily life at home are vital ties to building respect and understanding for one another. Having students teach each other about manners in their respective households is one such example (Vandeyar, 2017). These activities encourage students to really get to know their classmates.

Teach and Celebrate Diversity

Diversity in the classroom should not be thought of as an exceptional phenomenon but rather as a regular thing (Lissi et al., 2016). The success of inclusion depends on the teacher, beginning with the attitude and comfort level of differentiating instruction based on student need (Dimitrova-Radojchikj & Chichevska-Jovanova, 2015). Building an inclusive environment in the classroom begins with thoughtful lesson planning that considers each child's abilities and needs in mind, rather than adjusting a lesson as an afterthought. This allows each child to be fully included, rather than being an add on (Rusanescu et al., 2018).

It is useful to teach the benefits of accepting others by planning activities that specifically teach the concept. Lessons developed to express value in differences can be easily implemented by limiting the tools used for the lesson and then discussing how this affected the outcome of the work completed. Students might be asked to build a house using only one color or size block, color a picture using one crayon, or conduct a discussion about how there might only be one toy at the store. Activities such as these build critical thinking and reveal the necessity for variety. They can help clarify that just like there are differences in our blocks, crayons, and toys, there are also differences in how children learn.

Teachers need to know intervention strategies, how to incorporate all levels of Bloom's Taxonomy during instruction and be willing to experiment with project-based learning. Professionally, teachers who work collaboratively with other teachers in the field and implement peer coaching gain confidence with inclusive practices in the classroom (Bower, Van Kraayenoord, & Carroll, 2015). Cooperative learning is a versatile and useful tool that, when planned carefully and supervised closely, allows students to be equal partners in a project or problem-solving activity and individual strengths benefit the learning process for all involved (Gillies, 2016). Cooperative learning groups may be used to structure group projects by assigning roles and tasks that depend on all students contributing to meet the objective of the lesson (Gillies, 2016).

Teachers must first set the stage by creating a classroom where all students know one another by name, interact with one another by choice, and value the diversity within the class and group. This prevents students who are unsure of themselves, who tend to contribute less, and who engage at a much lower rate from having a less than satisfactory experience as the educator has ensured a sense of inclusiveness (Baloche, 2014). Class-wide peer-tutoring strategies are easily implemented once materials are made and organized and provide increased peer-to-peer interactions within a safe and structured activity (Ayvazo & Aljadeff-Abergel, 2014).

Other activities to build tolerance, understanding, and acceptance include role playing, puppetry, drama, movement, physical demonstrations, problem-solving discussions, games, art, music, language lessons, and conflict literature (Zepeda, 2014). Once students become engaged in the lessons and activities, friendships develop, and individuals realize they are more alike than different.

Zepeda (2014) tells of using story-telling and story-acting as a means of bringing together in friendship a diverse group of students. Students develop a cohesive community when they listen to one another because they become empathetic as they understand the needs of others. When given the opportunity, students will step up and take the leadership role through altruism (Zepeda, 2014) Although it is critical for the teacher to be warm and welcoming, when classmates act similarly, a classroom is not only a safe zone, it is a place where learning excels in an enriching and pleasurable way.

For older students, discussions about current tragedies such as hurricanes, tornadoes, wars, and fire recovery, researching laws and movies that address differences within populations, or situations that address remedies and produce inclusive mindsets give them a sense of being part of a community. Inviting guest speakers who may look, speak, behave, or believe differently to teach a lesson, tutor, talk about their life; or share a career, an experience, a food or a craft will also allow students to understand themes of diversity and acceptance (Zacarian & Silverstone, 2017). Most often these activities add to the current curricular content as a means to solidify knowledge, while visibly showing respect for differences.

Final Thoughts

Students who learn, look, speak, behave, or believe differently too often feel as if they do not belong, leading to lower self-esteem, lower expectations, and lower rates of success in learning. These students often begin to feel as if they do not belong in school. To advance the social standing of these students who are educationally at-risk, schools need to consciously and collaboratively work to build connections across four levels to include school-community, school-wide, classroom, and individual (Bower, 2015). Everyone within the system must use a common supportive language of acceptance and belief towards all members of the school community. Communicating school information in advance to the students and families indicates they are welcome and that the school is a shared space. Hosting family-centered activities that focus on student achievement in academics, the arts, and sports provides a showcase for all students. Embedding processes that promote social competence school-wide creates open, caring classrooms with activities planned to connect students to one another, leaving no one out. Making connections with various organizations from the community can offer unlimited opportunities to demonstrate that not only are all students an integral part of the school but also that they belong and are valued in the community. Supporting individual students and their families by connecting them to interventions and supports available both in and out of school is a vital component to inclusiveness.

Teachers have an obligation to create inclusive classrooms that welcome all and make every student feel valued. In order to address the acceptance of all students, educators' best approach is to tackle the core concepts by going beyond the walls of the classroom and school, into the community, school district, and so forth. To achieve inclusive schools, with a sense of acceptance and fairness, conscious change must be embedded in school improvement across all levels (Ainscow, Dyson, Goldrick & West, 2012).

Points to Remember

- *Classroom teachers have the responsibility and the influence to advance the social standing of students from educationally at-risk populations.*
- *Classroom teachers change how students who learn, look, speak, behave, or believe differently are valued within the class community.*

- *Welcoming diversity into the school and classroom begins with more than an attitude of tolerance, it begins with visual evidence that differences are recognized and accepted.*
- *Modeling acceptance is preceded by preparing the classroom and hallways physically with pictures, books, and artifacts displaying many differences, created with intent.*
- *Once the environment exhibits acceptance of differences and teachers show acceptance of all children, lessons must be prepared that allow collaboration to build community in such a way that all children learn diversity is wonderful.*
- *Intolerance toward anyone must be stopped when even the slightest negative comment is heard, or any adverse action occurs.*

References

Ainscow, M., Dyson, A., Goldrick, S., & West, M., (2012). Making schools effective for all: rethinking the task. *School Leadership & Management*, 1-17. DOI: 10.1080/13632434.2012.669648

American Psychological Association. (n.d.). *Individuals with Disabilities Education Act (IDEA)*. Retrieved from http://www.apa.org/about/gr/issues/disability/idea.aspx

Anderson, L., (2017). "I'm known": Building relationships and helping students construct counternarratives on the west side of Chicago. *Inner City Schools: Inequities and Inequalities, 673*(1), 98-114. DOI: 10.1177/0002716217723613

Ayvazo, S., & Aljadeff-Abergel, E., (2014). Classwide peer tutoring for elementary and high school students at risk: listening to students' voices. *Support for Learning, 29*(1), 76-92. DOI: 10.1111/1467-9604.12047

Baloche, L., (2014) Everybody has a story: Storytelling as a community building exploration of equity and access. *Intercultural Education, 25*(3), 206-215. DOI: 10.1080/14675986.2014.905240

Bateson, M.C. (1994). *Peripheral visions: Learning along the way*. New York, NY: HarperCollins.

Bower, J. M., van Kraayenoord, C., & Carroll, A., (2015). Building social connectedness in schools: Australian teacher perspectives. *International Journal of Educational Research, 70*, 101–109. DOI: 10.1016/j.ijer.2015.02.004

Boyd, M. P., Jarmark, C. J., & Edmiston, B., (2018). Building bridges: coauthoring a class handshake, building a classroom community. *Pedagogies: An International Journal, 13*(3), 330-352. DOI: 10.1080/1554480X.2018.1437731

Bricker, D. (1995). The challenge of inclusion. *Journal of Early Intervention, 19*(3), 179–194. DOI: 10.1177/105381519501900301

Bromberg, M., & Theokas, K., (2013). *Breaking the glass ceiling of achievement for low income students and students of color.* Education Trust: Washington. DC.

Dimitrova-Radojchikj, D., & Chichevska-Jovanova, N., (2015). Teacher's acceptance of students with disability. *Bulgarian Journal of Science Education, 24*(5), 647-656. Retrieved from https://www.researchgate.net/publication/283479260_Teacher's_acceptance_of_students_with_disability

Duchaine, E. L., & Fain, A. C., (2018). The Inclusive Classroom: All Students Engaged and Learning, In N.D. Young, E. Jean, & T.A. Ctiro, (Ed.), *Stars in the Schoolhouse: Teaching Practices and Approaches that Make a Difference,* pp. 31-52. Wilmington, Delaware: Vernon Press.

Epstein, J.L. & Sanders, M.G. (2019). *School, family, and community partnerships: Your handbook for action* (4th ed.). Thousand Oaks, CA: Corwin

Friend, M. & Bursuck, W. D., (2012). *Including students with special needs: A practical guide for classroom teachers* (6th ed.). Upper Saddle River, NJ: Pearson/Merrill.

Gay, G. (2018). *Culturally responsive teaching: Theory, research, and practice.* New York, NY: Teachers College Press

Gillies, R. (2016). Cooperative learning: Review of research and practice. *Australian Journal of Teacher Education, 41*(3), 39-54. DOI: 10.14221/ajte.2016v41n3.3

Grant, K.B. & Ray, J.A. (2016). *Home, school, and community collaboration: Culturally responsive family engagement.* Thousand Oaks, CA: SAGE

Hardy, I., & Woodcock, S., (2015). Inclusive education policies: Discourses of difference, diversity and deficit. *International Journal of Inclusive Education, 19*(2), 141-164. DOI: 10.1080/13603116.2014.908965

Hendrikx, M. M. H. G., Mainhard, T., Boor-Klip, H. J., & Brekelmans, M., (2017). Our teacher likes you, so I like you: A social network approach to social referencing. *Journal of School Psychology, 63,* 35-48. DOI: 10.1016/j.jsp.2017.02.004

Hestenes, L. L., & Carroll, D. E., (2000). The play interactions of young children with and without disabilities: Individual and environmental influences. *Early Childhood Research Quarterly, 15*(2), 229–246. DOI: 10.1177/0271121407311482

Heward, W. L. (2013). *Exceptional children: An introduction to special education* (11th ed.). Upper Saddle River, NJ: Pearson/Merrill.

Jean, E. & Rotas, G. (2019). Fostering growth in the classroom: Climate, culture and supports that make a difference. In N.D. Young, E. Jean, & T.A. Citro, *The Empathic Teacher: Learning and Applying the Principles of Social Justice Education to the Classroom,* pp. 18-40. Wilmington, DE: Vernon Press.

Lee, A.M. (2018). *Individuals with Disabilities Act (IDEA): What you need to know.* Retrieved from https://www.understood.org/en/school-learning/your-childs-rights/basics-about-childs-rights/individuals-with-disabilities-education-act-idea-what-you-need-to-know

Liou, D. D., Martinez, A. N., & Rotheram-Fuller, E., (2015). "Don't give up on me": Critical mentoring pedagogy for the classroom building students' community cultural wealth. *International Journal of Qualitative Studies in Education, 29*(1), 104-129. DOI: 10.1080/09518398.2015.1017849

Lissi, M. R., Iturriaga, C., Sebastián, C., Vergara, M., Henríquez, C., & Hofmann, S., (2016). Deaf and hard of hearing students' opportunities for learning in a regular secondary school in Chile: Teacher practices and beliefs. *Journal of Developmental and Physical Disability, 29*(1), 55-75. DOI: 10.1007/s10882-016-9495-z

Lombardi, J.D. (2016). *The deficit model is harming your students.* Retrieved from https://www.edutopia.org/blog/deficit-model-is-harming-students-janice-lombardi

Menesini, E. & Salmivalli, C. (2017). Bullying in schools: The state of knowledge and effective interventions. *Psychology, Health, & Medicine, 22*(1), 240-253. DOI: 10.1080/13548506.2017.1279740

Moreno, I. (2016). *Illinois schools eliminating zero-tolerance policies.* Retrieved from https://www.sj-r.com/news/20160918/illinois-schools-eliminating-zero-tolerance-policies

National Center for Education Statistics. (2018). The Condition of Education: Children and Youth with Disabilities. Retrieved from https://nces.ed.gov/programs/coe

Olszewski-Kubilius, P., & Clarenbach, J., (2014). Closing the opportunity gap program factors contributing to academic success in culturally different youth. *Gifted Child Today, 37*(2), 102-110. DOI: 10.1177/1076217514520630

Partridge, E.J. (2018). *Empathy in inclusive classrooms: Exploring prosocial behaviour through children's academic writing skills.* Retrieved from https://ir.lib.uwo.ca/cgi/viewcontent.cgi?article=7279&context=etd

Price, K. M, & Nelson, K. L., (2014). *Planning effective instruction: Diversity responsive methods and management* (5th ed.). Bellmont, CA: Wadsworth, Centage Learning.

Richardson, R. C., & Norman, K. I. (1997). "Rita dearest It's OK to be different": Teaching children acceptance and tolerance. *Journal of Humanistic Education and Development, 35*(4), 188-97. DOI: 10.1002/j.2164-4683.1997.tb00369.x

Richardson, E. V., Papathomas, A., Smith, B., & Goosey-Tolfrey, V. L., (2017). The psychosocial impact of wheelchair tennis on participants from developing countries. *Disability and Rehabilitation, 39*(2), 193-200. DOI: 10.3109/09638288.2015.1073372

Rothrock, R. M., (2017). Constructing a high-stakes community in the classroom: A case study of one urban middle school teacher. *The Educational Forum, 81*(4), 363-376. DOI: 10.1080/00131725.2017.1350240

Rudenstine, A., Schaef, S., & Bacallao, D. (2017). *Meeting students where they are.* Retrieved from https://www.inacol.org/wp-content/uploads/2017/06/CompetencyWorks-MeetingStudentsWhereTheyAre2.pdf

Rusanescu, A. G., Sora, A. M., & Stoicescu, M. (2018). Comparative study on approaching inclusive physical education from the perspective of alternative pedagogies. *Revista Romaneasca pentru Educatie Multidimensionala, 10*(1), 123-135. DOI: 10.18662/rrem/23

Schwarz, P. (2006). *From disability to possibility: The power of inclusive classrooms.* Portsmouth, NH: Allyn & Bacon.

Serin, H. (2017). *Teaching about respect and tolerance with presentations on cultural values.* DOI: 10.23918/ijsses.v3i4p174

Shore, K. (2017). *Tactics to prevent teasing.* Retrieved from https://www.educationworld.com/a_curr/shore/shore043.shtml

Sigman, M. L., Tackett, M. E., & Azano, A. P., (2016). Using children's picture books about autism as resources in inclusive classrooms. *The Reading Teacher, 70*(1), 111–117. DOI: 10.1002/trtr.1473

Sparks, S.D. (2016). *Teaching English-language learners: What does the research tell us?* Retrieved from https://www.edweek.org/ew/articles/2016/05/11/teaching-english-language-learners-what-does-the-research.html

Sreckovic, M. A., Schultz, T. R., Kenney, C. K., & Able, H., (2018). Building community in the inclusive classroom setting the stage for success. *Young Children,* 74-81.

Sullivan, A. L., Klingbeil, D. A., & Van Norman, E. R., (2013). Beyond behavior: Multilevel analysis of the influence of sociodemographics and school characteristics on students' risk of suspension. *School Psychology Review, 42* (1), 99-114.

U.S. Department of Education (2017). Participation in Education: Children and Youth with Disabilities (Chapter 2). Office of Special Education Programs.

United Nations Educational, Scientific, and Cultural Organization. (1994). *The Salamanca statement and framework for action on special needs education.* Retrieved from www.unesco.org/education/pdf/SALAMA_E.PDF - France

Vandeyar, S. (2017). The teacher as an agent of meaningful educational change. *Educational Sciences: Theory & Practice, 17,* 373–393. http://dx.doi.org/10.12738/estp.2017.2.0314

Vaughn, S., & Bos, C. S., (2012). Strategies for teaching students with learning and behavior problems (8th Ed). Upper Saddle River, NJ: Pearson/Merrill.

Walsh, B. (2017). *When testing takes over.* Retrieved from https://www.gse.harvard.edu/news/uk/17/11/when-testing-takes-over

Young, N.D., Fain, A., & Citro, T.A. (2019). *Creating compassionate classrooms: Understanding the continuum of disabilities and effective educational interventions* Wilmington, DE: Vernon Press

Young, N.D. & Jean, E. (2018). Penciling in parents: Making time for partnerships that count. In N.D. Young, E. Jean, & T.A. Citro, *Head to Heart: High Quality Teaching Practices in the Spotlight,* pp. 107-120. Wilmington, DE: Vernon Press

Zacarian, D., & Silverstone, M., (2017). Building partnerships through classroom-based events. *Educational Leadership, 75* (1), 13-18.

Zepeda, J., (2014). Stories in the classroom: Building community using storytelling and story-acting. *Canadian Children, 29* (2), 21-26.

Chapter Eight

Understanding and Addressing Bias in Classroom Assessment: Promoting Fairness Through Equitable Grading Practices

Nicholas D. Young, *American International College*

Dianne M. Young, *University of Massachusetts*

Grades are a normal and established component of elementary, secondary, and higher education in the United States. Students accept that their work is going to be evaluated by their teachers, and teachers understand that one of the critical elements of their job is to assign grades that are intended to measure students' knowledge of curricular content or progress toward meeting a particular pre-determined standard of achievement (ACT Government Education, 2016). Unfortunately, students and their parents often place a much higher premium on the final grade than they do on the actual learning that has occurred, which detracts from the primary goal of education. It is an understandable phenomenon, as grades can have a tremendous impact on a student's educational trajectory; yet, it may not be reasonable to condense a student's performance in a course, or entire educational experience at a high school or college, to one single letter or number. Questioning the validity of our grading system, Finkelstein (1913) wrote

> When we consider the practically universal use in all educational institutions of a system of marks, whether numbers or letters, to indicate scholastic attainment of the pupils or students in these institutions, and when we remember how very great stress is laid by teachers and pupils alike upon these marks as real measures or indicators of attainment, we can but be astonished at the

> *blind faith that has been felt in the reliability of the marking system. School administrators have been using with confidence an absolutely uncalibrated instrument... What faults appear in the marking systems that we are now using, and how can these be avoided or minimized?* (p. 1).

Though this was written over a century ago, it is just as relevant in the 21st century. Now teachers are required to undergo extensive training to enter and remain in the profession and must complete graduate-level coursework in things like pedagogy, curriculum development, child and adolescent psychology, school law, special education, and the curricular content areas.

Some prospective teachers may take a course related to designing assessments and rubrics for classroom use, but rarely do they receive instruction on how to evaluate student work and assign a representative grade to that work (Guskey, 2006). This aspect of teaching is typically learned on the job, often in complete isolation. There is no assurance that a B in American History from one teacher means the same thing as a B from another teacher in the same school, let alone one from another school district or state. With a grading system that is so fraught with inconsistencies, teachers struggle to decide how to assign grades to their students. Teachers must figure out how to maintain objectivity while completing a task that, in its very design, is highly subjective (Her, 2015; Strauss, 2009). It is likely that most teachers, at least initially, will rely to some degree on their own experience as students. They will remember the grading practices that felt fair and may try to mimic those and will avoid replicating those that seemed arbitrary or even discriminatory (Guskey, 2006).

Teacher grades are of critical importance to students. The compilation of several "low stakes" individual grades is used to arrive at a final course grade which may then influence decisions on future educational opportunities (van Ewijk, 2011). Any biases in teacher grading may unfairly help some students while harming others. For this reason, the assessment of student learning in the classroom is an important consideration in teaching for social justice (Kelly & Brandjes, 2008; Malouff, Stein, Bothma, Coulter & Emmerton, 2014). Teachers at all levels of education must strive to ensure that their grading procedures are explicit, clearly articulated, and free from bias.

Simply defined, bias in grading occurs when one student's work, which is of equal quality to that of another student, earns a different grade from the same teacher. The grade difference is based on factors that are irrelevant to the assignment itself and may be a result of a conscious or unconscious bias held by the teacher (Hardre, 2014; Malouff & Thorsteinsson, 2016). Unfortunately, all teachers are susceptible to allowing the subjectivity of grading to take their assessment of student work adrift from the intended standard of achievement; however, they must be prepared to defend their assessment practices to students, parents, colleagues, and administrators (Kelly & Brandes, 2008). Student grades are a relatively public aspect of classroom teaching, yet the process by which the teacher arrives at these grades may be somewhat less accessible.

Striving for social justice in classroom assessment requires that all teachers be willing to examine their own grading practices with a critical eye in search of any biases that have impacted their assessment of student work (Autin, Batruch, & Butera, 2015). Teachers must ask themselves if factors such as gender, race, attractiveness, classroom behavior, previous achievement, sibling performance, knowledge of family, etc. (knowingly or unknowingly) affect the assessment of a student's work on this particular assessment (Cornwell, Mustard, & Van Parys, 2013). Dover (2009) describes six principles of teaching for social justice in P-12 classrooms, the fifth of which requires that teachers "critique and employ multiple forms of assessment" (p. 509).

Sources of Grading Bias

Grading bias may occur as a result of the design and/or implementation of an assessment measure. One bias of this type is a mismatch between the design of an assessment and its purpose (Hardre, 2014). For example, if the purpose of an assessment is to evaluate a student's understanding of the human digestive system as demonstrated on a student-made poster, should the "visual appeal" be a factor in the grade? If the grading criteria are clearly articulated for the student and they include neatness and creativity, then scoring a student lower for messy work may not constitute bias on its own, provided the evaluation of the content of the poster is not negatively impacted by the lack of visual appeal. In this type of assessment, there is also a chance that reverse bias may occur if a student's poster is so artistic and beautifully presented that inferior content is overlooked and the student receives a higher score than is warranted.

Another concern is when the design of the assessment potentially impedes the student's ability to demonstrate the desired content knowledge, such as using an essay for assessing understanding of math concepts. In this scenario, grades may be biased based on a student's language skills rather than his/her command of the mathematics. That is not to say that using writing as an assessment tool in mathematics is necessarily inappropriate, but rather that the criteria for success must be clearly articulated for students.

A source of implementation bias that teachers must be cognizant of is based on the manner in which they score the assessment. Two teachers may arrive at very different scores for the same piece of student work using the same scoring rubric if their philosophical approaches are different. One teacher may approach the assignment assuming that it is of adequate quality and subtract points for errors or missing components, while another may score the assignment starting from zero and adding points for evidence of desired elements (Hardre, 2014). A student who approaches the task by "checking the boxes" and making certain that all the required tasks have been completed may score much better with the first teacher than the second, while a student who goes above and beyond the expectation will likely earn a higher score from the second teacher.

Another type of implementation bias may occur if the grading of student work is inequitable due to inadvertent inconsistencies in the teacher's grading process. If a teacher is interrupted in the middle of grading or becomes fatigued after scoring multiple tests or essays, the scores may become skewed (Hardre, 2014). Student handwriting may also be a factor. When a student's work is easy to read, a teacher is likely to read it more carefully and provide extensive feedback. The content of a barely legible paper may be superior, but the teacher may be unwilling to put the extra time into deciphering the messy "chicken scratch" to give the assignment a fair score.

Unfortunately, even when teachers are aware of alternative kinds of assessments that may allow for more equitable assessment of all students, they often feel restricted by the need to prepare students for large-scale state-mandated academic achievement testing. Research has shown that middle and upper-class students tend to fare better on standardized tests than their less affluent peers, and similar achievement gaps exist based on race (Kelly & Brandes, 2008). When teachers feel political pressure to prepare their students for these (possibly biased) tests, their own in-class assessments are more likely to be similar to the standardized tests.

Regardless of the grade level or subject matter they teach, all teachers must make daily choices about what to teach and how to assess what their students have learned, and the choices they make may have lasting effects on students' motivation to learn. Guskey (2006) asked public school elementary and secondary educators to recall the most positive and negative experiences with grades that they recalled from their days as students. Overwhelmingly, the positive experiences related to very challenging tasks for which the teacher provided targeted feedback which helped guide the students to outstanding achievement. The respondents reported that the tasks were very difficult and, even if not of particular interest to them, they felt a tremendous sense of accomplishment and pride in completing them (Guskey, 2006). A combination of high expectations and explicit criteria for achieving excellence was evident in the vast majority of the positive experiences reported (Guskey, 2006). Conversely, a significant number of the negative memories were of assignments for which the expectation was unclear (Guskey, 2006). These educators remember feeling that the grade they received was unfair when the scoring parameters seemed arbitrary.

A second and significant source of grading bias is related to the personal information that teachers have about their students. The results of a meta-analysis of research regarding bias in grading suggest that bias is more likely to occur when graders are cognizant of external and unrelated information about the student (Malouff & Thorsteinsson, 2016). The studies included in this meta-analysis were experimental in design, and the graders were not the students' classroom teachers (Malouff & Thorsteinsson, 2016). In these studies, it was hypothesized that when outside graders were provided with potentially biasing information about some of the students whose work they would assess, their overall grades would show favor toward one group (Malouff & Thorsteinsson, 2016).

The direction of this favor was dependent on the type of biasing information, for example, if the experimental group was given surnames typical of immigrants, bias against this group was hypothesized; if the experimental group was described as academically gifted, bias toward this group was expected (Malouff & Thorsteinsson, 2016). Most of the studies included in the analysis found evidence to support the initial hypothesis; however, a few showed what seemed to be a "reverse" bias taking effect, where the scorer was more lenient on one group (Malouff & Thorsteinsson, 2016). In either case, the overall results point to a bias effect created by external information that is irrelevant to the academic task being assessed.

In a classroom setting at the P-12 level, it is normal for a teacher to be privy to potentially biasing information about his/her students (Dover, 2009). Teachers generally have access to a great deal of student data through the district's student information system, including demographics, past academic history, or current grades in other courses. They also must be informed if a student receives any special education services so that they are certain to adhere to any accommodations required by the educational plan. Whether or not a student receives free or reduced lunch, has regular interaction with the school counselor for mental health concerns, or frequents the assistant principal's office to be disciplined for behavioral issues, are all potentially biasing pieces of information about a student of which a teacher may be aware. It is important that the teacher be able to compartmentalize this information and not allow it to impact how the student's academic work is evaluated.

Relational bias can occur as a result of the interpersonal relationships between students and their teachers. Rauschenberg (2014) found that differences in assessment and grading are frequently produced by teacher knowledge and beliefs about individual students. Relational biases can work in both directions. That is, if not carefully checked, teachers may disadvantage or favor certain students based on biases that are completely disconnected from the academic work being assessed. A student who shows a positive attitude toward the teacher or class, for example, may inadvertently be scored higher for the same work as a student who is difficult or appears unmotivated. Or if a teacher knows certain information about a student's family background, particularly if the student has had to overcome significant challenges in his/her life, there is often a tendency to adjust grades upward in an effort to keep the student motivated (Hardre, 2014).

Less experienced or less confident teachers, in particular, run the risk of being biased by having access to the grades a student received from previous teachers (Malouff & Thorsteinsson, 2016). This bias can work in either direction depending on the grades the student received in previous classes. Teachers lacking confidence in their grading may question a low mark they've given a student whose previous history shows only high marks in a particular subject area. Conversely, they may view their own grading as too lenient if they've given a high grade to a student whose academic history shows mostly low marks.

When teachers believe that a previous teacher provided more expert evaluation of a student's work, they may consciously or unconsciously align their own grades with the previously earned scores (Hardre, 2014). Biases in grading may occur as a result of teacher perception of students based on gender, race, socio-economic status, physical attractiveness, classroom behavior, or other non-academic qualities (Malouff & Thorsteinsson, 2016; Haeran & Cowling, 2008).

Strategies to Minimize Grading Bias

In order to maximize equity in grading, teachers must be honest about their own potential biases and take steps to counteract their effect. It is possible for P-12 teachers to minimize bias in grading by carefully examining their own grading practices, engaging in collaborative grading with colleagues and creating a professional culture in which grading practices are discussed freely and openly (ACT Government Education, 2016; The University of North Carolina at Charlotte, 2019). Teachers must be completely transparent with students and parents about their grading policies and procedures and be willing to respond to questions or concerns about their grading. When teachers are confident enough to allow students and/or parents to challenge their evaluation, student learning may actually be enhanced (Kelly & Brandes, 2008).

Strategies that teachers can use to minimize potential bias in grading include the use of multiple graders, spaced repeat scoring, blind scoring, scoring by section, and using extremely precise scoring rubrics (Hardre, 2014). These strategies are not all equally practical and may not be useful for all types of assignments, but even periodic use of some or all of them is likely to keep teachers more aware of their own (often unconscious) biases.

Multiple Graders

If a school is large enough, the use of multiple graders may be possible. When two or more teachers score the same assignments, any potential bias held by the classroom teacher will likely become evident, and the teacher can grade future assignments more fairly simply as a result of this awareness (Vanderbilt University, 2019).

Spaced Repeat Scoring

One way that an individual teacher may monitor his/her own bias in grading is to use spaced repeat scoring, where the teacher scores the assignment and records the grade on a separate paper, not on the assignment itself (The University of North Carolina at Charlotte, 2019). Then the assignment is set aside for a period of time, possibly several days or even a week, before the teacher scores it again and compares the second grade to the one that was assigned the first time. This strategy requires a somewhat significant passage of time between the students' completion of the assessment and the receipt of their score and therefore is not ideal if the teacher wants to provide relevant and timely feedback. Time permitting, it could be an excellent strategy for minimizing bias when scoring summative assessments, such as final exams or capstone projects.

Blind Scoring

The use of blind scoring, or keeping the students' identities unknown during the scoring, is a common strategy used in colleges. Students may be assigned an identification number to be used on all assignments, or the school may employ the use of bar code technology to reduce identity-based bias (Haeran & Cowling, 2008). These strategies are not as common in P-12 schools, where teachers tend to have a more personal connection to their students and far more opportunities to assess student work. A simple way for P-12 teachers to approximate blind scoring would be to have students write their names in a less prominent location, such as the bottom corner of the back page.

Scoring by Section

For lengthy assessments, a teacher can grade more consistently if the grading is done one section or page at a time (Vanderbilt University, 2019). This strategy can provide two important safeguards to unfair or biased grading. First, by concentrating on one section at a time, the teacher will more likely provide identical scores to work of equal caliber. Second, this method can also provide the advantage of blind scoring because as the teacher moves through an entire set of papers, the names of students will not be displayed on every page.

Using Precise Scoring Rubrics

This should be the easiest strategy to implement, provided that the rubrics are appropriate and precise. Rubrics can be an incredibly useful way to minimize the subjectivity in grading student work, but only if they use very precise language and are designed to accurately assess the level of desired knowledge the student demonstrates (Bull Schaefer, Chase, & Teets, 2017). Rubrics for open-ended assignments, such as essays, performance assessments, or projects, should be provided to students when the task is assigned so that the scoring criteria are clear (Bonefeld, & Dickhaeuser, 2018; Bull Schaefer et al., 2017). Rubrics, per se, are not as common for math tests, but modified versions can be used to assist teachers in focusing on the primary concepts being assessed while paying less attention to other non-critical student errors.

Grading Bias vs. Expectation Bias

The focus of this chapter is on bias in assessment, but it is important to note that other biases may impact student achievement even if the evaluation of student work is fair and equitable. Research has shown repeatedly that teacher expectations have a significant effect on student effort (Ouazad & Page, 2013; van Ewijk, 2011). If a teacher has a negative attitude toward a student based on non-academic characteristics, this attitude may be unintentionally communicated to the student through a change in behavior or reduced expectations (van Ewijk, 2011).

Students are sensitive to teacher expectations, and their level of academic achievement can be positively or negatively affected by their perception of the teacher's expectations of them (van Ewijk, 2011). Different expectations can be communicated by the type and frequency of questions asked of students during instruction, as well as the feedback provided. If teachers communicate differentiated expectations, students may perform tasks to meet their expectations, rather than achieving their potential. Teachers should engage in regular self-reflection and examination of their own instructional practices to make sure this type of bias is not occurring in their classrooms (Hytten, 2015; Martinez, 2015).

Final Thoughts

Assessment of students' academic learning is an inherently subjective task and therefore at risk of being affected by teacher biases, either consciously or unconsciously. Grades play a tremendous role in determining future academic opportunities for students; therefore, it is critical to social justice education that potential biases in grading be identified and minimized. Despite the fact that teachers in the United States are required to engage in significant preparatory schooling before becoming licensed educators, strategies for effective and unbiased classroom assessment are often overlooked. Teachers are frequently forced to develop and refine their assessment practices on-the-job, but without adequate self-reflection and collaboration with colleagues, they may remain unaware of biases that are impacting the equity of their grading. Teachers should utilize a variety of strategies to eliminate biases and feel confident that their assessment of student knowledge is fair and just.

Points to Remember

- *Fair and unbiased grading is an important aspect of teaching for social justice.*
- *Teachers may hold conscious or unconscious attitudes about students that are based on non-academic characteristics such as gender, race, physical attractiveness, socio-economic status, attitude and behavior, family history, etc.*

- Teachers must utilize a variety of strategies to eliminate or minimize bias in grading.
- Fair and unbiased grading procedures should be transparent. Students and parents must have a clear understanding of how student knowledge will be assessed.

References

ACT Government Education. (2016). *Teachers' guide to assessment.* Retrieved from https://www.education.act.gov.au/__data/assets/pdf_file/0011/297182/Teachers-Guide-To-Assessment.pdf

Autin, F., Batruch, A. & Butera, F. (2015). Social justice in education: How the function of selection in educational institutions predicts support for (non)egalitarian assessment practices. *Frontiers in Psychology, 6*(707), 1-13. DOI: 10.3389/jpsyg.2015.00707

Bonefeld, M. & Dickhaeuser, O. (2018). (Biases) grading of students' performance: Students' names, performance level, and implicit attitudes. *Frontiers in Psychology, 9*(481), 1-13. DOI: 10.3389/psyg.2018.00481

Bull Schaefer, R.A., Chase, N.M., & Teets, W.R. (2017). How to use common technologies to minimize perceptual biases when grading essays: A five-step process. *Jesuit Higher Education: A Journal, 6*(1), 97-109. Retrieved from https://epublications.regis.edu/cgi/viewcontent.cgi?referer=https://www.google.com/&httpsredir=1&article=1202&context=jhe

Cornwell, C., Mustard, D.B., & Van Parys, J. (2013). Noncognitive skills and the gender disparities in test scores and teacher assessments. *Journal of Human Resources, 48*(1), 236-264. DOI: 10.3368/jhr.48.1.236

Dover, A.G. (2009). Teaching for social justice and K-12 student outcomes: a conceptual framework and research review. *Equity & Excellence in Education, 42*(4), 507-525. DOI: 10.1080/10665680903196339

Finkelstein, I.E. (1913). *The marking system in theory and practice.* Baltimore, MD: Warwick & York, Inc.

Guskey, T.R. (2006). *"It wasn't fair!" Educators recollections of their experiences as students with grading.* Retrieved from https://files.eric.ed.gov/fulltext/ED492005.pdf

Haeran, J. & Cowling, J. F. (2008). The use of bar code technology in grading to improve student anonymity and reduce identity-based bias. *Marketing Education Review, 18*(1), 65-70. DOI: 10.1080/10528008.2008.11489027

Hardre, P.L. (2014). Checked your bias lately? Reasons and strategies for rural teachers to self-assess for grading bias. *Rural Educator, 32*(2), 17. Retrieved from http://epubs.library.msstate.edu/index.php/ruraleducator/article/view/126

Her, B. (2015). *Same rubric, different student: Subjective grading effects students in different ways.* Retrieved from http://www.nhsomniscient.com/2015/06/01/same-rubric-different-student-subjective-grading-affects-students-in-different-ways/

Hytten, K. (2015). Ethics in teaching for democracy and social justice. *Democracy & Education, 23*(2), 1-10. Retrieved from https://democracyeducationjournal.org/home/vol23/iss2/1/

Kelly, D.M. & Brandes, G.M. (2008). Equitable classroom assessment: Promoting self-development and self-determination. *Interchange: A Quarterly Review of Education, 39*(1), 49-76. DOI: 10.1007/s10780-008-9041-8

Malouff, J.M., Stein, S.J., Bothma, L.N., Coulter, K., Emmerton, A.J. (2014). Preventing halo bias in grading the work of university students. *Cogent Psychology, 1*(1), 988937. DOI: 10.1080/23311908.2014/988937

Malouff, J.M. & Thorsteinsson, E.B. (2016). Bias in grading: A meta-analysis of experimental research findings. *Australian Journal of Education, 60*(3), 245-256. DOI: 10.1177/0004944116664618

Martinez, M.A. (2015). Engaging aspiring educational leaders in self-reflection regarding race and privilege. *Reflective Practice: International and Multidisciplinary Perspectives, 16*(6), 765-776. DOI: 10.1080/14623943.2015.1095727

Ouazad, A. & Page, L. (2013). Students' perceptions of teacher biases: Experimental economics in schools. *Journal of Public Economics, 105*, 116-130. DOI: 10.1016/j.jpubeco.2013.05.002

Rauschenberg, S. (2014). How consistent are course grades? An examination of differential grading. *Education Policy Analysis Archives,* (22), p. 92. DOI: 10.14507/epaa.v22n92.2014

Strauss, V. (2009). *Grading of students too subjective, education expert finds.* Retrieved from https://www.cleveland.com/nation/index.ssf/2009/10/grading_of_students_too_subjec.html

The University of North Carolina at Charlotte. (2019). *Grading and testing.* Retrieved from https://teaching.uncc.edu/services-programs/teaching-guides/assessment-and-feedback/grading-and-testing

Vanderbilt University. (2019). *Grading student work.* Retrieved from https://cft.vanderbilt.edu/guides-sub-pages/grading-student-work/

Van Ewijk.R. (2011). Same work, lower grade? Student ethnicity and teachers' subjective assessments. *Economics of Education Review, 30*, 1045-1058. DOI: 10.1016/j.econedurev.2011.05.008

Chapter Nine

Teaching to the Common Core State Standards While Emphasizing Social Justice: Classroom Strategies and Practices That Work

Kristi L. Santi, *University of Houston*

Jacqueline Hawkins, *University of Houston*

Sara J. Jones, *University of Houston*

Social Justice is a term used in many different social and political situations. It is necessary, therefore, to provide a context for social justice as it relates to students with disabilities and those in marginalized groups, to review of the state of education in the United States, as well as to provide strategies and practices that support social justice for all students in the context of the Common Core State Standards (CCSS). As a precursor to the discussion, it is important first to operationalize the term social justice. As might be expected, there are several definitions of social justice and varying accounts of where the term originated. Some accounts date back over 2,000 years to Plato and Aristotle (Chroust & Osborn, 1942). These early philosophers discuss justice as taking two forms (a) moral justice, or virtue, and (b) equality, or 'fair mean' (Chroust, & Osborn, 1942). Other sources link the concept of social justice to an Italian priest in the 1840s who discussed a return to general justice but with a modernized application. Thus, the term 'social justice' was coined (Novak, 2009). Regardless of which time-period is referenced, or whether internet or historical sources are cited, when looking at the term social justice there is one element that remains constant, and that is the term 'common good.'

According to Merriam-Webster (2018a), social justice has a deceptively simple definition, "a state or doctrine of egalitarianism" (n.p.). This definition requires further clarification. In particular, it is necessary to define egalitarianism. Merriam-Webster (2018b) defines egalitarianism as "a belief in human equality especially with respect to social, political, and economic affairs" (n.p.). According to Novak (2009), however, one must distinguish between equality and equity. If the term equality is applied to the educational system, it advocates for the schools to provide all students with the exact same resources irrespective of the student needs. (Levitan, 2016) Essentially, equality may generate situations that are not for the common good. Equality in education may result in waste and inappropriate expenditures – a waste of both money and time. Alternatively, if the term equity is applied to the educational system, it advocates for schools to provide all students with the resources they need to learn (Levitan, 2016).

It is important, therefore, to ensure that consideration is given to the perspective of social justice using the lens of equity. Equity decisions that make sure that students designated under any category of special populations (e.g., underrepresented minorities, English learners, special education, immigrant status, gifted and talented) have access to the educational support they need in a way that makes sense for the students. Equity decisions for the common good.

The State of Education Prior to the Common Core State Standards

As the discussion moves from defining terms to the application of strategies in the classroom, there are two points to address (a) the state of education, and (b) the emergence of the Common Core State Standards (CCSS). To place the emergence of CCSS into perspective, one must first review the demographic shifts in education over several decades (since reporting began in 1972) and the impact of those shifts on the U.S. educational system by 2008.

According to the National Center for Education Statistics (Planty et al., 2008), there was a substantial increase in the proportion of students who were classified as racial/ethnic minorities from 22% in 1972 to 42% in 2006, while the number of students who spoke a home language other than English was 10.8 million in that same year – this number was up from 3.8 million in 1979. The number of students who were provided services in special education also saw an increase from 3.7 million in 1976 to 6.7 million in 2006 (Planty et al., 2008). While the demographics were changing in our public school system, the reading and math scores of students in the U.S., as measured by the National Assessment of Educational Progress [NAEP], were not consistently rising at any of the three grade levels for which data is collected (i.e., grades 4, 8 and 12)

(NAEP, 2007). According to the Programme for International Student Assessment [PISA] (OECD, 2007), when the focus was literacy the U.S. was performing below the average level of 17 countries and within the average level of another eight, only five countries were below the U.S. In 2008, the U.S. was deemed to be in a state of academic decline and had experienced a substantial demographic shift in the ethnic makeup, first language, and support need of students who attended public schools (Aud et al. 2010). A course correction was necessary, and the Common Core State Standards were the result.

Introducing the Common Core State Standards (CCSS)

Background

In an effort to improve the educational system throughout the United States, as well as keep students competitive in a global economy, three entities, The National Governors Association, the Council of Chief State School Officers, and Achieve, Incorporated came together to work on a path to improvement for the U.S. educational system. An executive summary of the report recommended five action steps to address the equity imperative (Jerald, 2008).

> ***Action 1**: Upgrade state standards by adopting a common core of internationally benchmarked standards in math and language arts for grades k-12 to ensure that students are equipped with the necessary knowledge and skills to be globally competitive.*
> ***Action 2**: Leverage states' collective influence to ensure that textbooks, digital media, curricula, and assessments are aligned to internationally benchmarked standards and draw on lessons from high-performing nations and states.*
> ***Action 3**: Revise state policies for recruiting, preparing, developing, and supporting teachers and school leaders to reflect the human capital practices of top-performing nations and states around the world.*
> ***Action 4.** Hold schools and systems accountable through monitoring, interventions, and support to ensure consistently high performance, drawing upon international best practices.*
> ***Action 5.** Measure state-level education performance globally by examining student achievement and attainment in an international context to ensure that, over time, students are receiving the education they need to compete in the 21st century economy* (Jerald, 2008, p. 6).

It is clear that equity and social justice play an important role in this process of changing the educational system and are both noted in the supporting documentation:

> *State leaders also should tackle "the equity imperative" by creating strategies for closing the achievement gap between students from different racial and socioeconomic backgrounds in each of the action steps above. Reducing inequality in education is not only socially just, it's essential for ensuring that the United States retain a competitive edge* (Jerald, 2008, p. 6).

Common Core State Standards Review

The need to review the educational system through the lens of equity and global competency began with a report in 2008 (Jerald, 2008). This report led the way for the development of the Common Core State Standards [CCSS] (Common Core State Standards Initiative, 2018). The website, which hosts the information regarding the development of the standards, along with the standards themselves, is maintained by the Council of Chief State School Officers (CCSSO) and the National Governors Association Center for Best Practices (NGA Center). According to the website,

> *the standards are (a) research- and evidence-based, (b) clear, understandable, and consistent, (c) aligned with college and career expectations, (d) based on rigorous content and application of knowledge through higher-order thinking skills, (e) built upon the strengths and lessons of current standards, (f) informed by other top performing countries in order to prepare all students for success in our global economy and society* (Common Core State Standards Initiative, 2018, n.p.).

The standards are available in two broad categories: English Language Arts/Literacy and Mathematics. The standards are designed to help place learning outcomes in a clear and transparent manner for parents and students so that they, along with the professionals in education, have a common understanding of expectations - hence have a community available to support learning (Common Core State Standards Initiative, 2018). Given the length of the standards, the exact standards are not addressed in this chapter, but a review of the language in the actual standards was analyzed for terminology regarding social justice and equity.

The CCSS and the corresponding College and Career Readiness Standards (CCRS) do not include the exact verbiage of either social justice or equity; however, the standards were written with the intent of helping parents and professionals to know how students should be performing at the end of each grade level, based on the most current research available (Mishkind, 2014). With these benchmarks in place, the community that helped to develop the standards also developed activities, lesson plans, and a space on the internet for the exchange of ideas (Thome, n.d.). The extensive efforts of each professional organization involved in the creation of the CCSS and CCRS supported professionals in education to develop and implement best practices that ensure learning occurs for all students; thus, the standards help professionals in education to advance socially just practices by learning various ways to teach the content that students must learn in order to be productive members of the global economy.

Common Core State Standards (CCSS) and Students with Disabilities

While a larger community designed the Common Core State Standards, concerns have been raised regarding equity issues as they relate to students with disabilities. In response, McLaughlin (2012) described six principles for educational leaders to consider regarding CCSS and students with disabilities to include

1. *Recognize that students with disabilities are a heterogeneous group and require individualized educational planning.*
2. *Distinguish between accommodations and modifications.*
3. *Support an environment and set expectations that teachers will understand and use evidence-based practices.*
4. *Augment end-of-year state assessments with a schoolwide assessment program that can measure progress and growth.*
5. *Understand and support the alignment of IEPs with the CCSS.*
6. *Hire and support the best special educators.* (p. 23)

Students with disabilities are a heterogeneous group; thus, there is no 'one size fits all' and, just like decisions about the needs of students in general education, every student with disabilities presents with a diverse set of needs (McLaughlin, 2012). This is an important reminder as professionals in education continue to work on inclusionary practices that inherently require equity to be applied on a daily basis, regardless of labels (Gleason-Peet & Santi, 2018).

IDEA Partnership, sponsored by the National Association of State Directors of Special Education (2012), has a webpage dedicated to the

Common Core along with one section dedicated to the CCSS and students with disabilities. The website also provides a section on tools to help professionals learn more about CCSS, assessment, collaborations, accommodations, and other guides (National Association of State Directors of Special Education, n.d.).

The Individual Education Program (IEP) is the driver of the modifications and/or accommodations that is mutually agreed upon as part of a contractual agreement by the parents or guardian, the professionals in education who work directly with the student, and the student when appropriate (Center for Parent Information & Resources, 2017). The same cannot be said for the larger group of students from special population categories such as, but not limited to, students who are classified as at-risk or those classified as underrepresented minorities. Ultimately, it is up to the profession to ensure that the implementation of strategies works for each student, regardless of label. Through an equity lens educators focus on the common good of each student and his or her unique needs.

The importance of equity and social justice appear in the teaching standards for many organizations. The Council for Exceptional Children (2015) provides ethical principles and professional practice standards for special educators. The first standard states "Maintaining challenging expectations for individuals with exceptionalities to develop the highest possible learning outcomes and quality of life potential in a way that respects their dignity, culture, language, and background" (Council for Exceptional Children, 2015, p. 1). The National Board for Professional Teaching Standards (2016), provide evidence of social justice from the lens of building a culture of respect and collaboration, which is embedded throughout the explanation of the five core propositions. Essentially, policy and educational organizations are focused on the same socially just approaches that target outcomes that are in the common good.

Social Justice for All

The Southern Poverty Law Center and its project Teaching Tolerance (2014) created social justice standards set in an anti-bias framework. The four domains, or standards, of this framework include (a) identity, (b) diversity, (c) justice, and (d) action, or as they abbreviate – IDJA, and then each is broken down by grade level groups (K-2; 3-5; 6-8; 9-12) with five outcomes per domain (The Sothern Poverty Law Center, 2014). A companion curriculum marries the rigor of CCSS, literature, and the anti-bias framework and "follows a 'backwards design' approach" (The Southern Poverty Law Center, n.d., p. 6).

The standards and curriculum provide teachers with research-based strategies; however, instead of using pre-packaged curricula, the Teaching Tolerance project provides teachers with the opportunities to teach key academic skills in the area of reading with content that is anti-bias and helpful for English learners (The Southern Poverty Law Center, 2014). Each social justice standard is aligned with the appropriate grade-level CCSS, and critical thinking is a cornerstone of the materials they provide teachers. As an upper-grade level example, one lesson relied on text from Article 1, Section 9 of the U.S. Constitution to teach three key concepts of identity, diversity, and justice (The Southern Poverty Law Center, 2014). The lessons include responses for all guided questions with the exception of opinions, and students are encouraged to respond openly and honestly, which helps them to acquire critical thinking skills along with the ability to hear a different point of view without rushing to judgment. This type of discourse is a valuable skill in any setting using any type of communication tool.

The Teaching Tolerance curriculum teaches critical academic and social skills, both linked to declines in the academic standing of the United States, in a way that provides students a more authentic learning experience (The Southern Poverty Law Center, 2014). The open access approach to the materials also sets these standards and associated teaching materials apart from other curricula. Combining the curriculum with classroom strategies that promote educational equity for all students regardless of race, disability, or economic status is a vital next step.

Combining Frameworks and Classroom Strategies

The Common Core State Standards were, in part, instituted to help educators address the equity imperative through the use of strategies to help close the achievement gaps (Jerald, 2008). While much has been written about academic success and the need to look at educational opportunities through the lens of student strengths while understanding and considering areas of need, taking all the information and practically applying it is not always easy (Santi, Hawkins, & Christensen, 2018). There are several frameworks in place with a research base that can be readily adapted to incorporate more equitable ways in which professionals in education can address the needs of all the learners in the classroom (CAST, 2018; Center for Applied Linguistics, 2018; IES: What Works Clearinghouse, n.d.). These frameworks and the resources provide a comprehensive, yet not inclusive, list of resources that professionals in education can use to learn more about positive ways in which they can build socially just and equitable practices into the daily lesson plans. In order to help ensure educational equity, strategies and resources are listed below each framework that focus on academic achievement as a way to build a society whereby all citizens can be positive contributors. While there are myriad strategies available, a sampling of options is provided as well as research-based documents that offer a more comprehensive list of individual strategies.

Universal Design for Learning (UDL)

In the past, teachers have often operated from a deficit model for students who did not reach the state benchmarks for academic success (Lombardi, 2018). The focus was on what the students lacked rather than ways in which models of equity could help move the students forward. In the ten years that have passed since the release of the *Benchmarking for Success* report (Jerald, 2008), more teacher education programs have dedicated space to teaching the Universal Design for Learning as one way to reach students from diverse backgrounds (CAST, 2018). UDL is a research-based framework that provides educators with multiple means of teaching to ensure they connect with the diverse students who are sitting in their classroom (CAST, 2018) Equally important, students are able to use a variety of methods to express themselves and demonstrate learning (CAST, 2018). Essentially, the overall goal of UDL is to develop expert learners who are purposeful and motivated, resourceful and knowledgeable, strategic and goal-directed and, consequently, teachers who support a more equitable approach to classroom planning (CAST, 2018). That said, the implied goal of UDL is to encourage educators to use their expertise to design and deliver instruction and assessments that support the common good.

Strategies. Technology provides educators with a way to deliver UDL lessons. When merging UDL, technology, and social justice standards, students can enrich their academic and social skills. The Office of Educational Technology developed a National Education Technology Plan to detail specific examples of how technology can help educational professionals, policymakers, and parents ensure equity and accessibility for all students (U.S. Department of Education, Office of Educational Technology, 2017).

Differentiated Instruction is another way in which educational professionals can create equitable learning experiences for students. For instance, if a teacher is using the UDL framework in conjunction with a Sheltered Immersion Observation Protocol (Echevarria, Vogt, & Short, 2008) lesson plan, that educational professional has thought through the content being delivered (what is being taught), in a manner that uses a variety of teacher tools and student skills (how) to allow the students equal but differing approaches to achieving the academic outcome (why). The what, how, and why, are the UDL multiple meaning concepts (CAST, 2018). This differentiation and flexibility in teaching provides all students with the appropriate level of scaffolding that ensures a socially just approach to the curriculum.

The Institute for Educational Sciences (IES)

The Institute for Educational Sciences (IES) (n.d.) through the portal What Works Clearinghouse, has released several guidebooks for working with diverse students. The practice guides include recommendations based on research and report out practices that have strong evidence, moderate evidence, or no-evidence in several areas including, but not limited to, reading, dropout prevention, behavior, math, and writing (Institute for Educational Sciences, n.d.). These are all resources that are publicly available and continually updated with the more recent practices. Ultimately, the IES guides provide a practical tool for educators to reduce inequality in the classrooms while maintaining the rigor and relevance required to remain competitive in a global economy (Institute for Educational Sciences, n.d.).

Strategies. When working through the Practice Guides offered by IES (n.d.), teachers can match the 'how to carry out the recommendation' to the social justice standards and lessons and, for middle and upper grades, to the College and Career Readiness Standards (Mishkind, 2014). As one example, recommendation three of the IES Practice Guide Summary: Foundational Skills (Foorman et al., 2016) is to *teach academic vocabulary in the context of other reading activities* (p. 8). The social justice standards, diversity #7 reads, *students will develop language and knowledge to accurately and respectfully describe how people including themselves are both similar to and different from each other and others in their identity groups* (The Southern Poverty Law Center, 2014, p. 3). A teacher can respond to both the IES recommendation and the social justice standard by using authentic experiences such as the lesson, "What is Community?" from the Teaching Tolerance (2018) website. Building these opportunities at the younger grades and carrying them through to high school graduation, we set our students up for success as they move to college and/or career by teaching them a skill set that will be vital to have in a global economy.

Sheltered Instruction Observation Protocol (SIOP)

The Sheltered Instruction Observation Protocol (Center for Applied Linguistics, 2018; Echevarria et al., 2008) is a research-based and validated framework for developing high-quality lesson plans that target all learners. The success of the model is that it provides teachers with a way to look at the lesson plans through the lens of the academic needs of each child in the classroom (Center for Applied Linguistics, 2018). There are eight interrelated components that, taken together, provide a clear, structured, delivery of the content so the students understand the objectives of the daily lesson from start to finish. These "eight interrelated components are (a) lesson preparation, (b) building background, (c) comprehensible input, (d) strategies, (e) interaction, (f) practice and application, (f) lesson delivery, and (g) review and assessment" (Center for Applied Linguistics, 2018, n.p.). When writing a lesson plan, using a model such as the one that follows, teachers have the opportunity to think about the curriculum materials and their students in a more meaningful and equitable manner.

Strategies. Lesson plans are the framework for the delivery of content each school day and serve as a road map whereby the educational professional has charted the course of instruction, allowing for any roadblocks and detours that might occur along the way. A smooth ride on this trip is one in which the lesson plan, such as the SIOP model, (Echevarria et al., 2008) has predetermined where the roadblocks may occur, much like an online mapping program does when individuals plan a real road trip. SIOP (Echevarria et al., 2008) has the teacher consider the audience (who is in the room) including students who have limited English proficiency and students from diverse cultural backgrounds. This can be accomplished by completing the content objective such as 'Students will be able to (behavioral verb) their knowledge of (concept/skill) by completing (demonstration of learning).' A second objective is written using the same format but this time the focus is on the language needed so that the student can appropriately engage with the academic content. Once these two objectives are clarified, vocabulary and background knowledge, which might be two potential roadblocks, are addressed (Center for Applied Linguistics, 2018). Teachers complete the lesson plan using an "I Do, We Do, You Do" model (Santi, 2015). At times, lesson planning has been considered a lost art in education; however, taking the time to think through roadblocks that students, and often the teacher, may find along an instructional path will help educators to think through lessons to ensure socially just practices are being utilized each day; thus, supporting a smoother journey through the educational system. A lesson framework such as the SIOP model (Echevarria et al., 2008) is one that can easily incorporate the Teaching Tolerance curriculum (The Southern Poverty Law Center, 2014).

Final Thoughts

In general, the information presented provides a review of the implementation of the Common Core State Standards (2018). Starting with the benchmarking report (Jerald, 2008), the state leaders from both political parties, saw the need to address what they deemed the equity imperative in an effort to make the United States public education system more socially just. From this, the CCSS and CCRS were developed and disseminated. Strategies and resources were presented to assist in the implementation of structuring schools to be more equitable in the approach to the teaching the curriculum. As reading is a conduit to the academic content in all other areas of education, it is important to highlight the strategies, such as those above, that have been compiled by researchers over the last 20 years, which highlight that students who go on to do well in college are generally those who are taught how to handle complex texts (ACT, 2006).

Parents, policymakers, and professionals in education can assist in the implementation of various strategies and approaches that will help teach tolerance, respect, and understanding for all in the educational community. The takeaway message is that when the educational approach incorporates a design that values and integrates diversity, such as UDL (CAST, 2018), using a tool that helps educators plan ahead for potential roadblocks, such as SIOP (Center for Applied Linguistics, 2018), along with teaching skill sets based on research, such as IES (IES: What Works Clearinghouse, n.d.), the educational system can work towards building a society that prepares all students to be active, positive contributors to our global society; thus, the educational system can support the common good.

Points to Remember

- *Equity is the goal of educational practices, providing students what they need to be successful.*
- *The CCSS was a derivate of the national drive of state leaders to address the 'equity imperative.'*
- *The CCSS were an attempt to provide a level playing field whereby all students and parents knew what the educational outcomes were by grade level.*
- *Planning ahead can help teachers move from a 'one-size-fits-all' approach to teaching.*
- *There is a multitude of resources readily available online and through books.*

References

ACT, Inc. (2006). Reading between the lines: What the ACT reveals about college readiness in reading. Iowa City, IA: Author. Retrieved from https://eric.ed.gov/?id=ED490828

Aud, S., Planty, M., Snyder, T, Bianco, K., Fox, M., Frolich, L. ...& Drake, L. (2010). *The condition of education 2010* (NCES 2010-028). National Center for Education Statistics, Institute of Education Sciences, U.S. Department of Education. Washington, DC. Retrieved from https://nces.ed.gov/pubs2010/2010028.pdf

CAST. (2018). Retrieved from http://www.cast.org/our-work/about-udl.html

Center for Applied Linguistics. (2018). *What is the SIOP model?* Retrieved from http://www.cal.org/siop/about/

Center for Parent Information & Resources. (2017). *The short-and-sweet IEP overview.* Retrieved from https://www.parentcenterhub.org/iep-overview/

Chroust, A-H., & Osborn, D.L. (1942). Aristotle's Conception of Justice, 17 Notre Dame L. Rev. 129. Retrieved from http://scholarship.law.nd.edu/ndlr/vol17/iss2/2

Common Core State Standards Initiative. (2018). *About the standards.* Retrieved from http://www.corestandards.org/standards-in-your-state/

Council for Exceptional Children. (2015). *Code of Ethics.* Retrieved from https://www.cec.sped.org/~/media/Files/Standards/Professional%20Ethics%20and%20Practice%20Standards/Code%20of%20Ethics.pdf

Echevarria, J., Vogt, M. E., & Short, D. (2008). *Making content comprehensible to English learners: The SIOP model* (3rd ed.). Boston, MA: Pearson/Allyn & Bacon.

Foorman, B., Beyler, N., Borradaile, K., Coyne, M., Denton, C. A., Dimino, J., ... & Wissel, S. (2016). *Foundational skills to support reading for understanding in kindergarten through 3rd grade (NCEE 2016-4008).* Washington, DC: National Center for Education Evaluation and Regional Assistance (NCEE), Institute of Education Sciences, U.S. Department of Education. Retrieved from https://ies.ed.gov/ncee/wwc/Docs/PracticeGuide/wwc_foundationalreading_040717.pdf

Gleason-Peet, C., & Santi, K.L. (2018). Barriers between the theory and implementation of inclusion and resources to remove these obstacles. In O'Connor, J. (Ed) *Cultivating Inclusive Practices in Contemporary K-12 Settings.*

Institute of Educational Sciences: What Works Clearinghouse. (n.d.). *Practice Guides.* Retrieved from https://ies.ed.gov/ncee/wwc/PracticeGuides

Jerald, C.D. (2008). *Benchmarking for success: Ensuring U.S. students receive a world-class education.* Retrieved from https://www.edweek.org/media/benchmakring%20for%20success%20dec%202008%20final.pdf

Levitan, J. (2016). The difference between educational equality, equity, and justice...and why it matters. *Forum of the American Journal of*

Education. Retrieved from http://www.ajeforum.com/the-difference-between-educational-equality-equity-and-justice-and-why-it-matters-by-joseph-levitan/

Lombardi, J.D. (2016). *The deficit model is harming your students.* Retrieved from https://www.edutopia.org/blog/deficit-model-is-harming-students-janice-lombardi

McLaughlin, M.J. (2012). Six principles for principals to consider in implementing CCSS for students with disabilities. *Principal,* 22-26. Retrieved from https://www.naesp.org/principal-septemberoctober-2012-common-core/access-common-core-all-0

Merriam-Webster. (2018a). *Social justice.* Retrieved from https://www.merriam-webster.com/dictionary/social%20justice

Merriam-Webster. (2018). *Egalitarianism.* Retrieved from https://www.merriam-webster.com/dictionary/egalitarianism

Mishkind, A. (2014). Overview: State definitions of college and career readiness. *College & Career Readiness & Success Center at American Institutes for Research.* Retrieved from https://ccrscenter.org/sites/default/files/CCRS%20Defintions%20Brief_REV_1.pdf

NAEP. (2007). The nation's report card: Reading 2007. Retrieved from https://nces.ed.gov/nationsreportcard/pdf/main2007/2007496.pdf

National Association of State Directors of Special Education (2012). *Common Core State Standards and students with disabilities.* Retrieved from http://www.ideapartnership.org/media/documents/CCSS-Collection/ccss-dg_4.pdf

National Association of State Directors of Special Education (n.d.). *Common Core State Standards and assessments collection: Tools.* Retrieved from http://www.ideapartnership.org/index.php?option=com_content&view=article&id=1522

National Board for Professional Teaching Standards (2016). *What teachers should know and be able to do.* Retrieved from http://accomplishedteacher.org/wp-content/uploads/2016/12/NBPTS-What-Teachers-Should-Know-and-Be-Able-to-Do-.pdf

Novak, M. (2009). *Social Justice: Not what you think it is.* Heritage Lectures. Retrieved from www.heritage.org/Research/Religion/hl1138.cfm

OECD. (2007). *PISA 2006: Science competencies for tomorrow's world: Executive summary.* Retrieved from https://www.oecd.org/pisa/pisaproducts/39725224.pdf

Planty, M., Hussar, W., Snyder, T., Provasnik, S., Kena, G., Dinkes, R. ... & Kemp, J. (2008). *The Condition of Education 2008* (NCES 2008-031). National Center for Education Statistics, Institute of Education Sciences, U.S. Department of Education. Washington, DC.

Santi, K.L. (2015). The journey to implementing best practices. *Journal of Education and Human Development, 4*(3), 33-41. Doi: 10.15640/jehd.v4n3a4

Santi, K.L., Hawkins, J.M., & Christensen, C. (2018). *Everybody belongs: Structuring positives environments.* In N.D. Young, C.N. Michael, and T.A.

Citro, (Eds.) *Emotions and Education: Promoting Positive Mental Health in Students with Learning Disabilities*, Vernon Press.

Teaching Tolerance. (2018). *What is community?* Retrieved from https://www.tolerance.org/classroom-resources/tolerance-lessons/what-is-community

The Sothern Poverty Law Center. (2014). *Teaching Tolerance Anti-bias Framework.* Retrieved from https://www.tolerance.org/sites/default/files/general/TT%20anti%20bias%20framework%20pamphlet_final.pdf

The Sothern Poverty Law Center. (n.d.). *Perspectives for a diverse America: A K-12 literacy-based anti-bias curriculum.* Retrieved from http://www.tolerance.org/sites/default/files/general/Perspectives%20for%20a%20Diverse%20America%20User%20Experience.pdf

Thome, C. (n.d.). *Bringing the Common Core Standards to the classroom.* Retrieved from https://www.readinga-z.com/research/bringing-the-common-core-standards-to-life-in-the-classroom.pdf

U.S. Department of Education, Office of Educational Technology. (2017). *Reimagining the Role of Technology in Education: 2017 National Education Technology Plan Update.* Washington, D.C. Retrieved from https://tech.ed.gov

Chapter Ten

College Preparation and Professional Development: What Every Preservice and Veteran Teacher Should Know About Social Justice Education

Nicholas D. Young, *American International College*

Jennifer Innocenti, *American International College*

The field of education is becoming more diverse as it evolves over time (Cambron-McCab & McCarthy, 2005; Ingersoll & Merrill, 2017; Villegas & Lucas, 2002). Cambron-McCabe and McCarthy (2005) raise questions about the efficacy of existing preparation programs and concerns regarding the extent that social justice is being considered in the development of new approaches in preparing future educators. Scholars have argued that the core teacher preparation curriculum needs to be largely intact while adding a few courses in multicultural education, bilingual education or urban education (Villegas & Lucas, 2002); however, Hytten (2015) argues that ethics and teacher foundations, which were salient to the foundations of learning to treating all students in an ethical and equal manner, are no longer part of teacher preparation education. While Villegas and Lucas (2002) note that adding the aforementioned courses does not extend far enough for teacher preparation in the education of diversity. The courses can be taught, yet there is no reinforcement in other courses, and there is limited encouragement to embrace diversity within their own belief system; therefore, the individual's own belief system can minimize or wash out what is taught about culturally responsive education.

Social Justice in Education Preparation

Social justice educators need to model socially acceptable tolerance and fairness to reduce microaggression and violence against students who do not identify in the dominant group. The education gap has led to a "political commitment to fairness and equal educational opportunity." (Cambron-McCabe & McCarthy, 2005, p. 202). The language set forth by the policy makers to address the achievement gap, however, has led to increasingly more controversial confrontations that address race, class, gender, sexual orientation, and systemic inequalities (Cambron-McCabe & McCarthy, 2005).

Villegas and Lucas (2002) note the importance of being aware that not all students identify with the dominant group, particularly due to migration from other countries. One in five students are poor; this translates into approximately 19 percent, while another 41 percent are low-income, according to Koball & Jaing (2018). As of 2003, 23 percent of students in P-12 schools were considered to be a racial or ethnic minority and, just over ten years later, that number has grown to approximately 30 percent (U.S. Department of Education, National Center for Education Statistics, 2015). Approximately one in five children, ages 5 to 17, speaks a primary language other than English (The Annie E. Casey Foundation, 2018). This multicultural trend continues to grow; therefore, a pressing issue has become how to prepare future teachers for the diversity of students who have racial, ethnic, social class, and English as a second language backgrounds (Villegas & Lucas, 2002).

Characteristics of a Culturally Responsive Educator

Future educators must articulate a construct of teaching and learning for themselves that addresses multiculturalism and diversity as a focal point or foundation rather than a dab of diversity here or there, and becoming culturally responsive begins in college (Alismail, 2016; Vescio, Bondy, & Poekert, 2009). Villegas and Lucas (2002) describe six characteristics that define a culturally responsive educator to include (1) socially conscious, (2) accepting of students from culturally diverse backgrounds, (3) self-confidence that they can bring about change and acceptance through education, (4) able to promote academic growth through understanding how the student constructs knowledge, (5) knows about the lives of their students, and (6) utilizes knowledge of student backgrounds to create and implement instruction; thus, encouraging learning beyond the bounds of family and community.

A socially conscious teacher is able to recognize that there are "multiple ways to perceive reality and that these ways are influenced by one's location in the social order" (Villegas & Lucas, 2002, p. 21). In order to achieve sociocultural consciousness, the educator must first be mindful that everyone they come into contact with (e.g., students and their families) will have their own way of thinking, behaving, and being and that these are influenced by an individual's race, ethnicity, socioeconomic status, social class, and language (Alismail, 2016; Vescio et al., 2009). Hytten (2015) notes that in order for individuals to understand the world around them, they must first examine their own sociocultural identity, ethics, and morals. This self-reflection must include a critical self-analysis (Hytten, 2015). Villegas and Lucas (2002) argue that during self-reflection, the future educator must explore the social and cultural groups that they belong to; especially those that identify the self by race, ethnicity, religious beliefs, social class, gender, and language. During self-reflection, the individual must critically analyze how each group has influenced personal beliefs and experiences (Hytten, 2015; Villegas & Lucas, 2002).

Public schools receive financial assistance from the state based on an antiquated funding formula (Chingos & Blagg, 2017). Higher taxed communities would provide more money/resources for the school, while poorer communities would not produce the same revenue/resources; thus, not every institution is treated equally within a state (Chingos & Blagg, 2017; Dover, 2009). In some cases, institutions further create unjust fairness and inequity by sorting the students based on merit (i.e., talent and effort). This may create inequity due to surmising that students with greater talents and effort deserve more benefits. This ideology reflects a dominant cultural belief that the students with greater achievements are pushed towards leadership opportunities and those that have lower achievements are pushed towards more menial opportunities (Mthethwa-Sommers, 2014). Villegas and Lucas (2002) argue that it is easier to blame the student for academic failure, rather than blame the institution for being impartial and discriminatory. All future educators, therefore, must gain sociocultural consciousness to identify the connection between institutions and society and the students that attend in favoring the privileged and oppressing the poor.

The second characteristic requires future educators to have an accepting attitude towards students with culturally diverse backgrounds (Villegas & Lucas, 2002). Educators inadvertently have the power to teach their students to conform to society or foster diverse viewpoints from that influence the way each individual learns, speaks, and behaves (Villegas & Lucas, 2002). Villegas and Lucas (2002) suggest that future educators that have the mindset that students of color, minorities, and English as a Second Language (ESL) learners already know about discrimination and may have experienced discrimination; therefore, educators should familiarize the dominant group with concepts that are culturally sensitive.

Educators who hold an accepting attitude towards students with culturally diverse backgrounds are able to show more support and compassion towards student achievement and foster different viewpoints and ways to learn, and model more appropriate behaviors to reduce microaggression and violence (Vescio et al. 2009; Villegas & Lucas, 2002). Villegas and Lucas (2002) argue that teacher expectations convey confidence in the students by exposing them to an intellectually rigorous curriculum, teaching strategies to help promote learning, accountability to high-performance expectations, encouragement to excel, and building cultural resources in the school. Ultimately, educators who display an accepting attitude towards students with culturally diverse backgrounds model tolerance, respect, and acceptance of the differing viewpoints.

A future social justice educator who has self-confidence can bring about change and acceptance through education. This third characteristic requires a teacher to strive towards growth and development of democratic citizenship through critical thinking, compassion, responsibility, open-mindedness, care, and respect (Hytten, 2015). Educators recognize that teaching is more than sharing information about certain subjects; rather, it is often driven by political and ethical obligations (Villegas & Lucas, 2002). Hytten (2015) argues that educators must remain neutral in their teaching; however, bias may be inadvertently conveyed through the texts chosen, teaching methods, activities / assignments, and grading policies. Teachers must select materials and resources that are geared toward cultural sensitivity.

Self-confident future educators see institutions and society as interconnected and recognize that teaching methods can challenge and transform inequalities among other students, or maintain the status quo (Villegas & Lucas, 2002). Villegas and Lucas (2002) point out that there are many factors that work against future teachers being socially just such as

> *hierarchical and bureaucratic nature of the education system, time pressure, insufficient opportunities for collaboration with others, resistance by those in positions of power to equity-oriented change, lack of personal understanding of oppression and empathy for those who are oppressed, and despair that change is possible* (p. 24).

Preservice educators need to believe that institutions can promote social reform, recognize that there may be failures in promoting fairness but also successes in change, and that change is a slow process (Alismail, 2016). In order to bring about change, the future educator needs to learn about the change process, obstacles to change, conflict resolution, and have a belief that schools can become more equitable (Alismail, 2016).

The fourth characteristic requires the preservice educator to understand how each individual constructs knowledge as a way to increase the student's ability to show academic growth (Villegas & Lucas, 2002). In a constructivist perspective, learning is accomplished through bringing about meaning from new ideas and experiences that occur at school (Bates, 2016). Students have various experiences that are derived from their social interaction at home, personal and cultural knowledge, family traditions, social interactions in the community and organizations, and their social interaction at school (Villegas & Lucas, 2002). In order to help students' challenge their own belief system, the teacher must engage individuals in questioning, interpreting, and analyzing information that is relatable as well as expose students to different personalities, cultures, and experiences (OECD, 2009). Due to differences in interpreting and understanding, teachers must consciously monitor the developing understanding of the new ideas unfolding and be ready to adjust the plan of action to meet the student's needs while building on the student's strengths (OECD, 2009).

In a constructivist view, students are perceived as capable learners who work hard to decipher new ideas (Bates, 2016). Student viewpoints based on the way they learn and perceive the world are seen as resources for further development rather than as problems that need to be corrected. Constructivist teachers are responsible for adjusting school standards to the varying backgrounds of the students in their class (Villegas & Lucas, 2002). The constructivist foundation of teaching is to promote critical thinking, collaboration, problem-solving, and recognition of different perspectives, and thus encouraging students to become participants in a democracy (Bates, 2016). Encouraging students to strive harder and promote problem-solving leads to academic tenacity (Villegas & Lucas, 2002). A constructivist view offers advancement to cultural sensitivity in the classroom, but it does not block out dominant forms of literacy that include the development of direct instruction, memorizing, and practice (Bates, 2016).

The fifth characteristic involves the teacher learning about the lives of the students in their care. Villegas and Lucas (2002) argue that the teacher must build bridges between the student's knowledge, experience, and new information. In order, to achieve the "bridge", the teacher must know the subject matter as well as the student's background outside of the classroom (Bernard, 2010). This concept further provides the teacher insight into how the student learns and promotes motivation by individualizing and tailoring the learning to individual environments (Villegas & Lucas, 2002). This is especially important to people of color and minorities who often need to see value in the school system based on people they know in society (Bernard, 2010).

Conducting home visits and interacting with students in the community (outside of the classroom) is one way to gain trust and insight into the culture and background of the family (Parent Teacher Home Visits, 2016). Teachers can hold parent-teacher conferences to check in with the parents/guardian to see how the student is doing at home, which helps to make learning at the student level more motivating and attainable through relatable material (Young & Jean, 2018).

The sixth characteristic requires the teacher to utilize personal knowledge of the student's background to create and implement instruction that encourages learning beyond the family and community (Villegas & Lucas, 2002). A teacher who is culturally responsive utilizes practices that promote the student's construction of knowledge, builds on personal and cultural strengths, helps students examine the curriculum from various viewpoints, uses varied assessment practices that promote learning, and makes the culture of the classroom inclusive for all students (Gay, 2018). Students have more interest in learning and retaining material that they feel is relevant to their lives rather than learning to memorize material, despite limitations based on personal non-dominant group diversity (Gay, 2018).

The Culturally Responsive Preservice Educator

The path to becoming culturally responsive begins with the college student who needs to learn a broad range of knowledge and skills, a thorough and comprehensive foundation of content knowledge based in the academic discipline of choice, an understanding of how the concepts relate to each other, a deep knowledge of the principles of inquiry, and the nature of discourse (Villegas, 2007). Villegas (2007) argues that future educators need to have a firm understanding of how children and adolescents develop and learn as a significant emphasis is placed on how the teacher-student relationship molds the outcome of the child, his or her behavior, academic success, and career influence.

Successful college preparation needs to foster developmental skills for creating a learning environment that will

- Build on the established individual strengths while stimulating the student through meaningful and purposeful activities;
- Make the subject matter not only relatable but interesting, captivating and alive; identifying methods to obtain and utilize community resources;
- Recognize the learning disabilities that could affect the students' learning and participation - learning a skill to teach to the mass then identify the students that are struggling and provide a stronger support system for growth;
- Monitor the learning development of their students;
- Effectively model socially acceptable behavior and re-directing ideas as needed;
- Utilize assessment practices; and
- Learn methods to create an inclusive classroom community (Villegas, 2007).

Becoming culturally sensitive begins in college preparation; future educators need to be consciously aware that in order to teach equitability they must identify and understand the barriers to learning such as race/ethnic minority, gender, or socio-economic status (OECD, 2009; Villegas, 2007).

College preparation courses need to encourage preservice teachers to act and behave in such a way that it will predict their future behavior when they graduate from college. This concept is derived from the learning theory that argues that a teacher's behavior is shaped by college preparation, schooling, and life experiences (Villegas, 2007). The preservice teacher's belief system can be a future barrier to not only teaching but influencing students. Many times, potential teachers enter college with the notion that students of color are lacking in developmental and fundamental ways; therefore, cultural diversity is a problem that needs to be overcome, in addition to teaching acceptance, fairness, and equity (Villegas, 2007).

Villegas (2007) referenced a study where preservice instructors had to guess the IQ and grade point average (GPA) of all the students in the class (which was mixed with Caucasian and African American students). The results indicated that the preservice instructors identified the African Americans students as having lower IQ scores, lower GPAs, lower self-confidence, less ambition, and less self-sufficient than the Caucasian students. Hytten (2015) argues that teachers need to remain neutral and check their biases, as having a negative view or stereotypical view of students based on race, gender, socio-economic status, orientation, religious, or ethnic background could lead to erroneous expectations as well as reduce student motivation and achievement (Villegas, 2007).

During preservice, future educators are tasked with completing supervised training in a P-12 classroom as a way to foster a personal vision of social justice education and teaching; learn to develop empathy for diverse students; nurture a personal notion for idealism; enhance their passion for shaping the lives of their students; promote social justice activism both inside and outside of the classroom; and continue to challenge negative beliefs about students of color (Brown, Lee, & Collins, 2014). To be culturally responsive, therefore, culturally sensitive preservice teachers must strive to learn as much about their students as possible to help facilitate learning.

Undergraduate coursework provides background information on various cultures; however, the future educator often does not comprehend how to make practical use of that knowledge and relate the material to culturally diverse students (Villegas & Lucas, 2002). Villegas and Lucas (2002) argued that differences exist with every individual, which influences the culture or group, creating ever-evolving, changing, and adapting conditions; therefore, no teacher can possibly learn "everything" about their students during one academic year.

The Culturally Responsive Veteran Teacher

Gunzenhauser (2015) argued that veteran teachers should, ideally, have more experience and practice than a preservice educator; however, this is not necessarily in the best interest of the educator or the student. The experiences that a veteran teacher has endured could lead to personal negative biases and problematic conclusions or ethical challenges about the populations they have educated. Veteran teachers may give up and/or become stagnant in their teaching due to a feeling that change is not being made. Other educators may feel they have mastered the art of social justice education and feel that they engage all students in a fair and equitable manner; however, upon reflection, the veteran teacher has become well versed in avoiding controversy rather than engaging the controversy (Gunzenhauser, 2015). Hytten (2015) suggested that teaching social justice education can create an uncomfortable learning environment; yet, it does promote democratic citizenship. A veteran teacher can help students move past polite conversation and guide them to productively challenge each other's viewpoints and beliefs in a safe and secure space (Gunzenhauser, 2015).

Social Justice Professional Development

Social justice education theory is perceived as a continuum, whereby educators benefit from a continuous examination of implications during each phase of their careers through teaching and administrator roles. Without regular continuing education courses, professionals can become stagnant in their mindset of what constitutes social justice. Policymakers, too, play an important role in promoting social justice. They should consider the importance of recruiting diverse candidates by ensuring that application processes and recruiting efforts attract minorities and members of marginalized and diverse populations. When possible, efforts need to be made to create pathways for alternate candidates as well. Some states (i.e. California) offer expedited courses in education to prepare social justice leaders to hold administrative positions through rigorous testing rather than direct experience in the classroom and coursework; and still others, like Florida, have removed the credentialing process for school administrators to broaden the candidate pool (Cambron-McCabe & McCarthy, 2005).

Final Thoughts

Preservice teachers must go through a rigorous training program that examines social justice from a variety of angles to include race, gender, poverty, and any other form of discrimination. Using the six characteristics suggested by Villegas and Lucas (2002) as well as using college coursework, teacher leaders, and professional development will aid in curbing any outward expressions of non-culturally responsive ideology. Making an extra effort to get to know the students in the classroom will improve teaching and provide a platform for open and clear communication between teacher and student, teacher and family, as well as between students. Regardless of the path chosen, the importance of preparing social justice leaders for the future cannot be overstated. To achieve this goal, teachers, administrators, and policymakers alike will need to stress ongoing education, inclusive policies, and the promotion of social justice to ensure that educators and leaders represent diverse populations, points of view, and stakeholders.

Points to Remember

- *Future educators are exposed to social justice education when they first attend school in P-12.*
- *During college, future educators must reflect on their own beliefs, experiences, and perceptions to become culturally responsive.*
- *There are six characteristics that define a culturally responsive educator to include (1) social consciousness, (2) an accepting attitude of students with culturally diverse backgrounds, (3) self-confidence that they are a change agent of acceptance through education, (4) promotes knowledge through understanding how the student constructs knowledge, (5) knows about the lives of his or her students, and (6) utilizes personal knowledge of the student's background to create and implement instruction to encourage learning beyond one's family and community.*
- *Future educators must have a broad range of knowledge and skills, and a thorough comprehension of the academic disciplines.*
- *Educators' expectations influence the academic outcome of their students, as well as influence their learning process.*
- *Not being aware of one's biases and negativity could lead to lower expectations and lower academic scholarship of one's students that further affect self-esteem and motivation.*
- *Preservice educators need to find appropriate supervision that fosters social justice education learning.*
- *Veteran educators must not become stagnant in their teaching methods; rather they must evolve with the social justice continuum and build democratic citizenship through modeling.*
- *States are moving to expand the concept of social justice in their administration and are eliminating education experience for an administrative role. Recruiting is geared towards women, people of color, individuals with a non-education-based degree, and fast-track programs that focus on rigorous testing rather than coursework.*

References

Alismail, H.A. (2016). Multicultural education: teachers' perceptions and preparation. *Journal of Education and practice, 7*(11), 139-146. Retrieved from https://files.eric.ed.gov/fulltext/EJ1099450.pdf

Bates, B. (2016). *Learning theories simplified: And how to apply them to teaching.* Thousand Oaks, CA: SAGE

Bernard, S. 92010). *Science shows making lessons relevant really matters.* Retrieved from https://www.edutopia.org/neuroscience-brain-based-learning-relevance-improves-engagement

Brown, A.L., Lee, J., & Collins, D. (2014). Does student teaching matter? Investigating pre-service teachers' sense of efficacy and preparedness. *Teaching Education, 26*(1), 77-93. DOI: 10.1080/10476210.2014.957666

Cambron-McCabe, N., & McCarthy, M.M. (2005). Educating school leaders for social justice. *Educational Policy, 19*(1), 201-222. DOI: 10.1177/0895904804271609

Chingos, M.M. & Blagg, K. (2017). *Making sense of state school funding policy.* Retrieved from https://www.urban.org/sites/default/files/publication/94961/making-sense-of-state-school-funding-policy_0.pdf

Chung, R.C.Y. & Bemak, F.P. (2012). *Social justice counseling: the next steps beyond multiculturalism.* Thousand Oaks, CA: Sage.

Dover, A.G. (2009). Teaching for social justice and K-12 student outcomes: a conceptual framework and research review. *Equity & Excellence in Education,42*(4), 507-525. doi: 10.1080/10665680903196339

Gay, G. (2018). *Culturally responsive teaching: Theory, research, and practice.* New York, NY: Teachers College Press

Gunzenhauser, M.G. (2015). Enacting social justice ethically: individual and communal habits. *Democracy & Education, 23*(2), 1-6.

Hytten, K. (2015). Ethics in teaching for democracy and social justice. Democracy & Education, 23(2), 1-10

Ingersoll, R., & Merrill, L. (2017). *A quarter century of changes in the elementary and secondary teaching force: From 1987 to 2012. Statistical analysis report* (NCES 2017-092). U.S. Department of Education. Washington, DC: National Center for Education Statistics. Retrieved from https://nces.ed.gov/pubs2017/2017092.pdf

Koball, H. & Jiang, Y. (2018). *Basic facts about low-income children.* Retrieved from http://www.nccp.org/publications/pub_1194.html

Mthethwa-Sommers, S. (2014). *Narratives of social justice.* New York, NY: Springer

OECD. (2009). *Creating effective teaching and learning environments: First results from TALIS.* Paris, France: OECD.

Parent Teacher Home Visits. (2016). *Why home visits?* Retrieved from http://www.pthvp.org/what-we-do/why-home-visits/

The Annie E. Casey Foundation. (2018). *Children who speak a language other than English at home.* Retrieved from https://datacenter.kidscount.org/data/tables/81-children-who-speak-a-language-other-than-english-at-home#detailed/1/any/false/871,870,573,869,36,868,867,133,38,35/any/396,397

U.S. Department of Education, National Center for Education Statistics. (2015). *State nonfiscal survey of public elementary/secondary education.*

2003-04 and 2013-14. Retrieved from
https://nces.ed.gov/programs/digest/d15/tables/dt15_203.70.asp

Vescio, V., Bondy, E., & Poekert, P.E. (2009). Preparing multicultural teacher educators: Toward a pedagogy of transformation. *Teacher Education Quarterly, 36*(2) 5-24. Retrieved from https://www.jstor.org/stable/23479249

Villegas, A.M. (2007). Dispositions in teacher education: a look at social justice. *Journal of Teacher Education,* 58(5), 370-380. doi: 10.1177/0022487107308419

Villegas, A.M., & Lucas, T. (2002). Preparing culturally responsive teachers: rethinking the curriculum. *Journal of Teacher Education,* 53(1), 20-32.

Young, N.D. & Jean, E. (2018). Penciling in parents: Making time for partnerships that count. In N.D. Young, E. Jean, & T.A. Citro, *Head to Heart: High Quality Teaching Practices in the Spotlight,* pp. 107-120. Wilmington, DE: Vernon Press

List of Acronyms

AAVE	African American Vernacular English: a form or linguistic capital not viewed as proper English.
ESEA	Elementary and Secondary Education Act: A law enacted in 1965 to eliminate gaps in education due to poverty.
ESSA	Every Student Succeeds Act: The 2015 reauthorization of the Elementary and Secondary Education Act that included more guidance on family engagement and added other measures to ensure student success.
CASEL	Collaborative for Academic, Social and Emotional Learning: website geared to high-quality, evidence-based social-emotional learning that supports leaders, policymakers, and educators.
CCRS	College and Career Readiness Standards: These address the skills students need to acquire prior to graduation in order to be productive members of a global society.
CCSS	Common Core State Standards: Details the required knowledge for each grade level in math and English language arts.
FAPE	Free and Appropriate Public Education: all children in the United States are guaranteed a free education, with equal access to all children, that is appropriate to their needs.
GLSEN	Gay, Lesbian and Straight Education Network: group and website dedicated to creating safe spaces in schools for all students.
GPA	Grade Point Average: a number that represents all grades acquired over time.
IDEA	Individuals with Disabilities Education Act: Originally named the Education for All Handicapped Children Act of 1975, this improved the education services for students with disabilities
IEP	Individualized Education Plan: A legal document that ensures specialized instruction for students with disabilities
IES	Institute for Educational Sciences: Run by the U.S. Department of Education, IES
IQ	Intellectual Quotient: a number that expresses an individual's intelligence on a continuum.

LGBTQ	Lesbian, Gay, Bisexual, Transgender, Queer: The acronym is used to describe those who are gender non-conforming. Sometimes also referred to as LGBTQ+.
LRE	Least Restrictive Environment: ensuring that students with disabilities are not segregated; rather, they are taught in as close proximity to their non-disabled peers as possible.
NAEP	National Assessment of Education Progress: An assessment that represents what students in the United States know and can express in a variety of subjects.
NCFA	National Council for Adoption: A group that strives to meet the needs of all those involved in adoption.
NCLB	No Child Left Behind: The 2002 reauthorization of the Elementary and Secondary Education Act that required each state to determine the standards of success for Students and be held accountable for student growth.
P-12	Preschool to Grade 12: The school continuum of primary, middle, and secondary Education.
PBIS	Positive Behavioral Interventions and Supports: A means to encourage good behaviors through the use of positive incentives.
PISA	Programme for International Student Assessment: a measure of the abilities of students across fifteen member countries of the OECD (Organization for Economic Cooperation and Development).
SEL	Social-Emotional Learning: a way in which adults and children build skills to understand and manage emotions. It has become a framework used in the classroom to address the needs of children.
SIOP	Sheltered Instruction Observation Protocol: Research-based and validated framework for developing high-quality lesson plans that target all learners.
UDL	Universal Design for Learning: Research-based frameworks that provide educators with multiple means of teaching diverse students.
U.S.GAO	Government Accountability Office: Provides auditing, investigation, and evaluation services for Congress.

About the Primary Authors

Nicholas D. Young, PhD, EdD

Dr. Nicholas D. Young has worked in diverse educational roles for more than 30 years, serving as a teacher, counselor, principal, special education director, graduate professor, graduate program director, graduate dean, and longtime psychologist and superintendent of schools. He was named the Massachusetts Superintendent of the Year, and he completed a distinguished Fulbright program focused on the Japanese educational system through the collegiate level. Dr. Young is the recipient of numerous other honors and recognitions including the General Douglas MacArthur Award for distinguished civilian and military leadership and the Vice Admiral John T. Hayward Award for exemplary scholarship. He holds several graduate degrees including a PhD in educational administration and an EdD in educational psychology.

Dr. Young has served in the U.S. Army and U.S. Army Reserves combined for over 34 years; and he graduated with distinction from the U.S. Air War College, the U.S. Army War College, and the U.S. Navy War College. After completing a series of senior leadership assignments in the U.S. Army Reserves as the commanding officer of the 287th Medical Company (DS), the 405th Area Support Company (DS), the 405th Combat Support Hospital, and the 399th Combat Support Hospital, he transitioned to his current military position as a faculty instructor at the U.S. Army War College in Carlisle, PA. He currently holds the rank of Colonel.

Dr. Young is also a regular presenter at state, national, and international conferences; and he has written many books, book chapters, and/or articles on various topics in education, counseling, and psychology. Some of his most recent books include *The Burden of Being a Boy: Bolstering Educational and Emotional Well-Being in Young Males* (under contract); *Creating Compassionate Classrooms: Understanding the Continuum of Disabilities and Effective Educational Interventions* (2019); *The Special Education Toolbox: Supporting Exceptional Teachers, Students, and Families* (2019); *The Empathic Teacher: Learning and Applying the Principles of Social Justice Education to the Classroom* (2019); *Educating the Experienced: Challenges and Best Practices in Adult Learning* (2019); *Securing the*

Schoolyard: Protocols that Promote Safety and Positive Student Behaviors (2019); *Sounding the Alarm in the Schoolhouse: Safety, Security and Student Well-Being* (2019); *The Soul of the Schoolhouse: Cultivating Student Engagement* (2019); *Embracing and Educating the Autistic Child: Valuing Those Who Color Outside the Lines* (2019); *From Cradle to Classroom: A Guide to Special Education for Young Children* (2019); *Captivating Classrooms: Educational Strategies to Enhance Student Engagement* (2019); *Potency of the Principalship: Action-Oriented Leadership at the Heart of School Improvement* (2018); *Soothing the Soul: Pursuing a Life of Abundance Through a Practice of Gratitude* (2018); *Dog Tags to Diploma: Understanding and Addressing the Educational Needs of Veterans, Servicemembers, and their Families* (2018); *Turbulent Times: Confronting Challenges in Emerging Adulthood* (2018); *Guardians of the Next Generation: Igniting the Passion for Quality Teaching* (2018); *Achieving Results: Maximizing Success in the Schoolhouse* (2018); *From Head to Heart: High Quality Teaching Practices in the Spotlight* (2018); *Stars in the Schoolhouse: Teaching Practices and Approaches that Make a Difference* (2018); *Making the Grade: Promoting Positive Outcomes for Students with Learning Disabilities* (2018); *Paving the Pathway for Educational Success: Effective Classroom Interventions for Students with Learning Disabilities* (2018); *Wrestling with Writing: Effective Strategies for Struggling Students* (2018); *Floundering to Fluent: Reaching and Teaching the Struggling Student* (2018); *Emotions and Education: Promoting Positive Mental Health in Students with Learning* (2018); *From Lecture Hall to Laptop: Opportunities, Challenges, and the Continuing Evolution of Virtual Learning in Higher Education* (2017); *The Power of the Professoriate: Demands, Challenges, and Opportunities in 21st Century Higher Education* (2017); *To Campus with Confidence: Supporting a Successful Transition to College for Students with Learning Disabilities* (2017); *Educational Entrepreneurship: Promoting Public-Private Partnerships for the 21st Century* (2015); *Beyond the Bedtime Story: Promoting Reading Development during the Middle School Years* (2015); *Betwixt and Between: Understanding and Meeting the Social and Emotional Developmental Needs of Students During the Middle School Transition Years* (2014); *Learning Style Perspectives: Impact Upon the Classroom* (3rd ed., 2014); and *Collapsing Educational Boundaries from Preschool to PhD: Building Bridges Across the Educational Spectrum* (2013); *Transforming Special Education Practices: A Primer for School Administrators and Policy Makers* (2012); and *Powerful Partners in Student Success: Schools, Families and Communities* (2012). He also co-authored several children's books to include the popular series *I am Full of Possibilities*. Dr. Young may be contacted directly at nyoung1191@aol.com.

Elizabeth Jean, EdD

Dr. Elizabeth Jean has served as an elementary school educator and administrator in various rural and urban settings in Massachusetts for more than 20 years. As a building administrator, she has fostered partnerships with staff, families, various local businesses, and higher education institutions. Further, she is currently a graduate adjunct professor at the Van Loan School of Education, Endicott College and previously taught at the College of Our Lady of the Elms. In terms of formal education, Dr. Jean received a BS in education from Springfield College; an MEd in education with a concentration in reading from the College of Our Lady of the Elms; and an EdD in curriculum, teaching, learning, and leadership from Northeastern University.

Dr. Jean is a primary author on *The Burden of Being a Boy: Bolstering Educational and Emotional Well-Being in Young Males* (under contract); *The Empathic Teacher: Learning and Applying the Principles of Social Justice Education to the Classroom* (2019); *From Cradle to Classroom: A Guide to Special Education for Young Children* (2019); *The Potency of the Principalship: Action-Oriented Leadership at the Heart of School Improvement* (2018); *Dog Tags to Diploma: Understanding and Addressing the Educational Needs of Veterans, Servicemembers and their Families* (2018); *Stars in the Schoolhouse: Teaching Practices and Approaches that Make a Difference* (2018); *From Head to Heart: High Quality Teaching Practices in the Spotlight* (2018); *From Lecture Hall to Laptop: Opportunities, Challenges and the Continuing Evolution of Virtual Learning in Higher Education* (2017). She has also written book chapters on such topics as emotional well-being for students with learning disabilities, post-secondary campus supports for emerging adults, parental supports for students with learning disabilities, home-school partnerships, virtual education, public and private partnerships in public education, professorial pursuits, technology partnerships between P-12 and higher education, developing a strategic mindset for LD students, the importance of skill and will in developing reading habits for young children, and middle school reading interventions to name a few. Additionally, she has co-authored and illustrated several children's books to include *Yes, Mama* (2018), *The Adventures of Scotty the Skunk: What's that Smell?* (2014), and the *I am Full of Possibilities* Series for Learning Disabilities Worldwide. She may be contacted at elizabethjean1221@gmail.com.

Teresa Allissa Citro, PhD

Dr. Citro is the Chief Executive Officer, Learning Disabilities Worldwide, Inc. and the Founder and President of Thread of Hope, Inc. She is a graduate of Tufts New England Medical School and Northeastern University, Boston. Dr. Citro has co-edited several books on a wide range of topics in special education, and she co-authored a popular children's series *I Am Full of Possibilities*. She is the co-editor of two peer review journals including *Learning Disabilities: A Contemporary Journal and Insights on Learning Disabilities* from *Prevailing Theories to Validated Practices*. She is the mother of two beautiful children and resides in Boston, Massachusetts.

www.ingramcontent.com/pod-product-compliance
Lightning Source LLC
Chambersburg PA
CBHW052025290426
44112CB00014B/2381